Declutter Your Home

THE KELSIE'S WAY TO A CLUTTER FREE LIFE

A Workbook about Tidying, Cleaning and Organizing Your House, Room by Room, on a Daily, Weekly, Monthly and Seasonal Basis

KELSIE ZARIA

© **Copyright 2020 Kelsie Zaria - All rights reserved.**

The content contained within this book may not be reproduced, duplicated or transmitted without direct written permission from the author or the publisher.

Under no circumstances will any blame or legal responsibility be held against the publisher, or author, for any damages, reparation, or monetary loss due to the information contained within this book. Either directly or indirectly.

Legal Notice:

This book is copyright protected. This book is only for personal use. You cannot amend, distribute, sell, use, quote or paraphrase any part, or the content within this book, without the consent of the author or publisher.

Disclaimer Notice:

Please note the information contained within this document is for educational and entertainment purposes only. All effort has been executed to present accurate, up to date, and reliable, complete information. No warranties of any kind are declared or implied. Readers acknowledge that the author is not engaging in the rendering of legal, financial, medical or professional advice. The content within this book has been derived from various sources. Please consult a licensed professional before attempting any techniques outlined in this book.

By reading this document, the reader agrees that under no circumstances is the author responsible for any losses, direct or indirect, which are incurred as a result of the use of information contained within this document, including, but not limited to, — errors, omissions, or inaccuracies.

CONTENTS

INTRODUCTION	8
PART 1: DEEP CLEANING	10
CHAPTER 1 - DEEP CLEANING INSTRUCTIONS BY ROOM	12
KITCHEN CLEANING	12
Dusting	13
Cabinet Cleaning	15
Appliances (Microwave, Stovetop, Oven, Dishwasher)	17
Sink and Garbage Disposal	21
Kitchenware and Utensils	23
Clean Out the Drawers	24
The Refrigerator	25
The Freezer	26
Pantry	27
Garbage Can	29
Countertops and Backsplash	30
Kitchen Table and Chairs	31
Sweep, Vacuum, and Mop	33
KITCHEN CHECKLIST	35
LIVING SPACES	38
Pick Up Things That Don't Belong	38
Clean Furniture or Upholstery	38
Disinfect	39
Dusting	40
Curtains, Pillows, and Blankets	41
Vacuum, Sweep, or Mop	42
LIVING ROOM CHECKLIST	43
THE OFFICE	45
Dusting	45
Disinfect	45
Floors	47
OFFICE CHECKLIST	48
BATHROOM CLEANING	49
The Shower	49
The Toilet	52
The Sink, Faucet, and Countertops	53

Declutter Your Home - The Kelsie's Way to a Clutter Free Life

    Mirror, Trash Can, Rugs, and Bath Mats _____ 54
    The Vent and Floors _____ 55
BATHROOM CHECKLIST _____ 56
BEDROOM CLEANING _____ 58
    Dust and Disinfect _____ 58
    Bedding and Headboard _____ 59
    The Mattress _____ 60
    Floors, Rugs, and Trash _____ 60
BEDROOM CHECKLIST _____ 62
LAUNDRY ROOM _____ 63
    The Washer _____ 63
    The Dryer _____ 64
    The Sink, Countertops, and Shelves _____ 65
    Windows and Floors _____ 65
LAUNDRY ROOM CHECKLIST _____ 66
CHILDREN'S BEDROOM OR PLAYROOM _____ 68
    Dust and Disinfect _____ 68
    Clean the Floors _____ 69
CHILDREN'S ROOM CHECKLIST _____ 70
ENTRY SPACE AND DOORS _____ 71
    Doors _____ 71
    Shoes and Coat Rack _____ 73
    The Staircase _____ 73
ENTRY SPACE CHECKLIST _____ 75

PART 2: DECLUTTER AND ORGANIZATION _____ 76

CHAPTER 2 - DECLUTTER AND ORGANIZE BY ROOM _____ 78

THE KITCHEN _____ 78
    The Pantry _____ 78
    Pots and Pans _____ 80
    Containers and Measuring Cups _____ 81
KITCHENWARE _____ 82
    Plates, Cups, Silverware, and Cookware _____ 82
    Utensils and Tools _____ 83
    Kitchen Knives _____ 84
REFRIGERATOR AND FREEZER _____ 85
KITCHEN ORGANIZATION CHECKLIST _____ 86
CLOSETS _____ 88

Bedroom Closet _____ 88
Children's Closet _____ 90
Medicine Cabinet and Linens _____ 91
Cleaning Closet _____ 93
CLOSET CHECKLIST _____ 94
THE OFFICE _____ 96
Sorting and Storing _____ 96
The Desktop _____ 98
OFFICE CHECKLIST _____ 99
THE GARAGE _____ 100
GARAGE CHECKLIST _____ 102

PART 3: LISTS _____ 103

CHAPTER 3 - DAILY, WEEKLY, AND MONTHLY LISTS _____ 104

DAILY LIST _____ 104
WEEKLY GUIDE - 10 MINUTE ROUTINES _____ 106
MONTHLY LISTS _____ 108

CHAPTER 4 - SEASONAL AND DEEP CLEANING LISTS _____ 118

THE ULTIMATE DEEP CLEANING _____ 120

CHAPTER 5 - ALL ABOUT CLEANERS _____ 124

WHAT YOU SHOULD KNOW _____ 125
NATURAL CLEANERS - PRINTABLE LISTS _____ 128

CHAPTER 6 - MOVING GUIDE AND CHECKLIST _____ 137

MOVING INSTRUCTIONS _____ 138
MOVING CHECKLIST BY ROOM _____ 142
WHAT TO PACK _____ 143
MOVING ITEMS TO KEEP HANDY _____ 147

CHAPTER 7 - DECLUTTERING TECHNOLOGY _____ 149

HOW TO DECLUTTER YOUR COMPUTER AND PHONE _____ 149
Computer or Laptop _____ 149
Cell Phone _____ 150
TOP 10 DECLUTTER AND ORGANIZATION APPS _____ 153

CONCLUSION _____ 155

Introduction

Maintaining order and cleanliness in a home can be challenging. With busy schedules and long work days, the cleanliness of a home is not always the first priority. Homes that are not well kept can be a headache to clean. Clothes, dishes, and clutter seem to take over. Tasks become overwhelming and it feels like it will take an eternity to clean your home. After a long week, many prefer to spend time doing fun activities, hobbies, or visiting loved ones instead of cleaning and organizing.

With the help of this guide, we'll show you how and where to start deep cleaning and organizing your home. Cleaning your home doesn't have to be stressful and can be done little by little or all at once, if you prefer. This guide will give detailed instructions, provide the order in which to do tasks, and give helpful advice that will stick with you long after reading this guide. We'll take you through a detailed deep clean and provide daily, monthly, and yearly checklists to help you stay on top of it. Each and their specific items will be discussed so you know exactly how to clean and maintain them.

In addition, we'll provide instructions on how to make eco-friendly, do-it-yourself, affordable, and multipurpose safe cleaners. We'll take you through the risks of using harsh chemicals and show you easy alternatives. Using natural cleaners will keep you, your family, and the environment in good health. Once you've accomplished the deep cleaning portion, this guide will move into the second part: decluttering your home and organization.

Maintaining a clutter free, organized home is just as important as maintaining a clean home. When a home is disorganized, keeping spaces clean becomes a harder task. Spot cleaning is almost impossible when clutter lines the insides of cabinets and closets. Clutter makes items hard to find and crowds useful storage space that could better serve your needs. If your home doesn't have a lot of space, this guide will give helpful information on how to create space with detailed suggestions. The checklists, labeling advice, and detailed instructions given in this guide will help you create a better organization system that will be easy to create, maintain, and save time. Small space issues, too much space disorganization, and everything in between will be addressed.

We've included helpful lists for every scenario and preference. There's a list to guide you through deep cleaning your home, maintaining the home, how to sort through items in each room, seasonal cleaning, moving advice, do it yourself cleaners, and much more!

After reading this guide, you can look forward to a clean and organized environment that will allow proper relaxation and rejuvenation. You'll feel fully prepared and well informed on how to keep your home clean and organized. At the end of the book, you'll find 10 minute daily checklists that will help you manage weekly cleaning. The short lists will help you keep your home clean so you can spend more time doing what you enjoy!

PART 1: DEEP CLEANING

***

    This section of the book will take you through the deep cleaning process of your home. Each section is divided by room. The kitchen, living area, office, bathrooms, bedrooms, laundry room, garage, children's room, and entry space will all be discussed. Each section will explain how to clean the items most common to the specific room, but be aware that some of these items may be present in other rooms. You can use advice from other sections where applicable!

    You'll notice homemade cleaning solutions scattered throughout the sections. A list will be provided at the end of the book. The list will specify which cleaners are safe for which surface. Any cleaners mentioned throughout the book will also be repeated in that section for easy reference. The cleaning section later on in the book not only features helpful lists, but will give insight as to how home cleaners affect your health and the environment. Vinegar and baking soda will be mentioned frequently throughout this section. Vinegar and baking soda will be further addressed in the cleaning portion of the guide. Both make excellent natural cleaners. You'll be able to throw away any toxic cleaners and free up tons of space as many of the DIY cleaners are multipurpose!

    The lists are located after each section covering a specific room. It's suggested that you print each list and the cleaners list for easy access. You can store the list in their specific room and use it for reference in the future! Don't be afraid to print a few as you'll want to mark off each task with a check mark.

A deep cleaning can take a bit of time. Depending on your preference, you may wish to completely deep clean the entire home before moving onto the declutter section of the book. Or, you can deep clean a specific room and jump to the declutter section for the same room if you wish. You can find a monthly cleaning list that will take you through cleaning and decluttering tasks throughout the year in the lists section of this guide. However, try to set time aside to deep clean as much as possible in a shorter period of time. For you, maybe this means tackling the bottom floor of your home one weekend and the second floor the next!

This guide will give useful advice to make sure you only have to deep cleaning your home every so often. Keep in mind that a deep clean involves performing each task as thoroughly as possible and that it is more important than completing it quickly. A thorough deep clean will prevent you from doing the task repeatedly. If you're ready to enjoy a clean, stress free environment, then let's get started!

CHAPTER 1 - Deep Cleaning Instructions by Room

Kitchen Cleaning

The kitchen is one of the most important areas of a home. A kitchen is like the soul of a home. Not only is it where food is prepared, but also where family gathers. Memories and delicious food are all enjoyed from the work done in the kitchen. With so many elements needed to create a delicious meal, keeping the kitchen clean can be difficult. Dishes often pile up and crumbs linger, especially with a busy schedule. Unlike other rooms, each element has to be cleaned and ready to go at all times to ensure sanitation.

With this step by step program, deep cleaning your kitchen will be easier than ever. After a deep clean, maintaining the kitchen will become second nature and will allow more time for other activities. Each element of the kitchen will be discussed and directions on how to clean them efficiently will be given.

Dusting

Dusting may seem like a simple chore, but the reasons to dust the kitchen and home are endless. First, dust is created by small particles of dead skin cells, animal dander, bugs, hair, fibers, pollen, and other substances. When thinking of dust in this fashion, the reasons why dust shouldn't be in the kitchen are quite clear. Dust can settle in many places and can be hard to see in most cases. Dust can cause allergies and sickness because yes, dust contains germs. With movement, dust is able to travel and in a kitchen environment, this could mean it's getting into food. If you haven't considered this, it's possible that a lot of dust is floating in your kitchen currently. But not to worry, after a deep clean, maintaining a dust-free zone will be simple.

Step One:

Focus on the highest points of the kitchen. Dust will likely fall or spread, so it's best to leave the low points for last. This ensures all dust is removed from the kitchen. Decide the highest point of the kitchen and use a ladder, chair, or counter to stand on. Be safe and ask for help if needed. For many, the highest point of the kitchen will be on top of the cabinets.

Before dusting the top of the cabinets, it may be necessary to clean them first. If the tops have any residue, try this trick to clean them up. Place vinegar into a spray bottle and generously spray onto the tops of the cabinets. Sift baking soda over top of the vinegar and allow this to sit for a few minutes. You will notice the mixture fizzing and bubbling. Next, take an old credit card or a store card and scrape the tops of the cabinets. Use paper towels as necessary to wipe off the sediment on the card. Repeat this until the tops are clean and wipe them with a damp towel afterwards.

If only dusting is needed, use a microfiber cloth, natural dusting solution, a vacuum, or wipes to dust the tops of the cabinets. A toothbrush or paintbrush may also be helpful to dust any small, hard to reach areas. Be aware that the goal is to dispose of the dust, and not push it around.

Tip ☆

After dusting, cut and place wax paper to fit the tops of the cabinets. The wax paper will help catch roaming dust and ensure fast cleaning in the future. Newspaper or magazine pages also work and are a more sustainable option. With either method, be careful when removing these pages to keep the dust from floating off the paper.

Step Two:

After dusting the tops of the kitchen, it's possible some dust has fallen onto the cabinets or floor. However, any additional dust will be removed later on. One spot to pay extra attention to, in regards to dust, is the top of the refrigerator.

Using the same solution above, repeat the method used before if the top of the refrigerator contains grime. Otherwise, for a natural cleaner, mix one part vinegar and one part warm water and use a cloth to wipe down the top of the refrigerator. You can also continue this on the outer parts of the refrigerator to dust and clean the outside.

Step Three:

Although a more extensive section will be discussed later on how to clean windows, consider using the same vinegar solution to wipe down the window sills. This is another likely place dust collects.

Cabinet Cleaning

Step One:

Cleaning the outside and inside of kitchen cabinets will have a huge result on how clean your kitchen looks. Sparkly and pristine cabinets are a must, as they visually make up most of the kitchen.

Focus on cleaning the outer parts of the cabinets first. Over time, a buildup of grime and dirt can occur on the surface of cabinets. To clean wooden cabinets, create a natural mixture using:

- 1 cup water (237 mL)
- ½ cup white vinegar (118 mL)
- 2 tablespoons of olive oil (30 mL)
- 10 drops essential oil (lemon)
- 5 drops essential oil (cedarwood)

Mix the ingredients into a glass spray bottle and spray the surface. Allow the mixture to rest on the surface for 30 seconds. Use a microfiber cloth to wipe the surface. Not only will this clean the cabinets, but will also give them a nice polish with a fantastic aroma.

If your cabinets are not made of wood, consider using this recipe below to clean and polish. Mix the following into a glass spray bottle:

- 1 cup water (237 mL)
- ½ cup white vinegar (118 mL)
- 2 teaspoons of olive oil
- 10-15 drops essential oil (orange, lemon, etc.)

Step Two:

After cleaning the outside of the cabinets, turn the focus to the inside. Remove plates, bowls, or anything being stored. Begin wiping down the cabinets using one of the recipes above. Cleaning the insides of the cabinet will eliminate dust, dirt, and germs.

Step Three:

Because cabinet handles are often touched, they could be harboring a lot of germs. It's important to keep these surfaces clean especially when a household member is sick. Imagine touching a dirty handle and then grabbing utensils or plates. The kitchenware that was clean, now has the germs that originated from the cabinet handle. This step is quick, but very important.

Use a disinfectant wipe or spray and wipe each handle using a paper towel or cloth. After the cabinet handles are completed, continue cleaning the handle of the microwave, refrigerator, freezer, kitchen door knob, or any other handle in sight that's often touched. White vinegar, alcohol, such as rubbing alcohol or vodka, and essential oils are wonderful natural disinfectants that you probably have already.

Tip ☆

Turn on the exhaust fan immediately when cooking. Not every kitchen has this equipment but be sure to utilize it if you do. This will prevent any buildup or grease that stems from smoke or humidity coming off the stovetop.

Appliances (Microwave, Stovetop, Oven, Dishwasher)

Step One: Microwave

When cleaning the microwave, it's important to realize that a natural cleaner is best. Exposing food to chemicals may be damaging to health. Luckily, the microwave can be cleaned efficiently without using chemicals. Many microwaves become dirty over time by splattering and popping food. Cleaning out the microwave can be a daunting task because most of the food left is dried and hard to clean out. With this method, little to no effort is required and cleaning out the microwave is easy.

Start by adding half a cup (118 mL) of water to a glass, liquid measuring cup. Next, squeeze a medium sized lemon into the water and place the remaining lemon parts into the beaker. Place the measuring cup into the microwave and microwave for three minutes. Then, allow the beaker to sit in the microwave for an additional five minutes with the door shut. After five minutes, remove the glass plate and measuring cup. With a dry cloth, wipe out the microwave. This shouldn't take long since the lemon did most of the work. Don't forget the bottom, top, sides, and door of the microwave. Use the cloth to wipe off the glass plate and place it back in the microwave. This process should take under 10 minutes and is a foolproof method to a clean microwave! Don't forget to wipe down the outer parts of the microwave as well.

Tip ☆

The best way to keep a microwave clean is to cover any food placed in the microwave. This can be done by purchasing a microwave-safe cover from the store, paper towels, or better yet, a glass baking dish. Covering food will eliminate the need to clean the microwave drastically.

Step Two: Stovetop

Whether you have a gas or electric stove top, it's likely this is one of the first areas to accumulate left over food and crumbs. Keeping a stovetop clean can be difficult even when being careful. Cleaning the stovetop can be an easy task when the right solutions are used. No more agressive scrubbing or working up a sweat!

For a gas stove, there's a lot of nooks and crannies that crumbs can get into. Depending on how your stovetop looks at the start, it might be best to start with a vacuum. Start by removing the gas burner covers. Set them in a sink and fill the sink with hot water and dish soap. Next, set the vacuum next to the stove and use the vacuum hose to eliminate large debris. This step should take care of most of the crumbs not plastered onto the stovetop. Because a vacuum hose has a smaller opening, really get into each gas burner as much as possible. After vacuuming crumbs and debris, make a solution of baking soda and water. The texture should be paste-like, so start by adding as little water as possible to get the necessary thick consistency. Spread the mixture onto the stovetop. Avoid getting too close to the burners as it's not advised to get moisture in the burners themselves. Allow the paste to sit on the stovetop for 20 minutes before using a sponge to remove the paste. Rinse the sponge and rinse the surface with water. Be sure that you are using a delicate sponge to avoid scratches. By this time, you should be able to take a cloth or sponge and rinse the gas burner covers that were soaking. Get as much debris off of them and then return to the stovetop after drying.

For a glass top stove, spray the surface with one part water and one part vinegar. Allow this to sit on the stovetop for 10-15 minutes and then wipe away using a cloth.

Step Three: Oven

Although some ovens have a self-cleaning feature, it's always good to get in there yourself for a good clean. It is also the opinion of some that the self-cleaning feature is not thorough and can actually damage or hurt the longevity of oven racks. In addition, many report the self-cleaning feature is a smelly process. Luckily, cleaning the oven can be quite simple and natural products can be used. Use half a cup (90 grams) of baking soda and a dab of water to create a thick paste in a bowl. Spread the paste all over the inside of the oven and coat the walls. Try to avoid the heating elements in the oven usually located at the bottom and top. Depending on the dirt in the oven, gloves may come in handy. Coat the oven as evenly as possible using a circular motion. Allow the mixture to sit in the oven overnight. Allowing this will prove less work the following day. After the paste has done its work overnight, take a damp dish towel and begin to wipe and remove the mixture from the oven. Scrubbing is not necessary at this point. Fill a spray bottle with vinegar and spray onto all areas inside the oven. You should hear the baking soda and vinegar reacting. After about 30 seconds, use the damp dish towel to remove the rest of the mixture. Your oven should be looking pretty clean at this point! Do a final wipe down with a clean, damp dish towel to remove anything left behind.

To clean the oven racks, fill a bathtub or large sink with hot water. Fill it up enough so that the oven racks are covered with water. Add 1 cup (237mL) of dish soap to the tub or sink and let the racks soak overnight. The following day, use a towel to remove any left behind grease with scrubbing motions. This step shouldn't be too difficult or time consuming since the racks soaked overnight. A toothbrush may also come in handy for this step to really scrub and get every angle. After the racks are scrubbed, be sure to rinse them with water again before returning them to the oven.

Next, it's time to clean the oven glass. This step only takes about three or four minutes and is super effective. Open the oven door completely so that it's laying down flat. Most oven doors are able to do this. Pour one cup (237mL) of warm water onto the glass and sprinkle a generous amount of baking soda over top. After one minute, ball up a piece of aluminum foil to gently exfoliate the surface of the glass. The mixture should clear up any grease or grime with a little exfoliation. Use a paper towel, sponge, or cloth to remove the solution and rinse the glass with water again before drying.

Step Four: Dishwasher

If you're fortunate enough to have a functioning dishwasher, you know how helpful they can be to save time. Although dishwashers are generally pretty clean, there are a few extra steps that should be completed about every three months or during a deep cleaning.

First, remove the rack at the bottom of the dishwasher and inspect the drain. Make sure there is no debris hanging around in this area.

Next, remove the spray arm carefully. Inspect the spray arm and take notice of any grime. To remove any grime from the surface, dip a toothbrush in white vinegar and scrub the surface. Because a toothbrush has tiny little bristles, the toothbrush should be able to get into any holes as well to clean them out. After cleaning the spray arm, place the arm and rack back into the dishwasher.

Set a dishwasher safe bowl on top of the first rack in the dishwasher faced upwards. Fill the bowl with white vinegar and run the dishwasher on the highest possible heat setting.

Afterwards, generously sprinkle baking soda on the bottom of the dishwasher. You shouldn't have to remove the bottom rack again, but be sure to roll it out at least halfway to properly coat the bottom of the dishwasher. Like before, run a complete cycle on the hottest setting.

After these steps, your dishwasher should be pristine!

Sink and Garbage Disposal

Step One:

What many don't know is that the kitchen sink can harbor a lot of bacteria. Bits of food and dirt have a way of staying in the sink much longer than you might expect, producing tons of germs and bacteria.

To clean a stainless steel sink, create a paste using baking soda and water. Baking soda is great for a stainless steel sink because it will gently exfoliate the steel without scratching it. Spread the paste all over the sink and allow the paste to sit for 10 minutes. Then take a spray bottle of vinegar and spray the sink. Use a microfiber cloth and water to wash away the paste. Vinegar is a natural disinfectant and can also remove any water stains present. To get a little extra sparkle, drench a cloth with club soda or a little olive oil and rub it into the sink. Be sure to give the sink a final rinse with warm water.

Tip ☆

Don't leave sponges or any dish cleaning tools in the stainless steel sink. This is a common practice to dry out the sponge when not in use. This habit can make the surface underneath the sponge dull and even promote rusting. In addition, do not leave steel or iron cookware in the sink for a long period of time as this can lead to rusting and stains.

Composite or stone sinks are often beautiful and can last a long time. Granite, limestone, soapstone, and marble are common materials in a stone sink. These four materials are porous, meaning overtime, oils and dirt are able to penetrate the surface causing stains, so it's important to keep the sink clean. For a quick clean, mix one part water and one part white vinegar and scrub the sink using a non-abrasive sponge. After rinsing the sink, apply cooking oil such as olive oil all over the sink, using a cloth. Allow the oil to sit in the sink for one or two minutes before removing it with a microfiber cloth.

Copper sinks can be cleaned similarly using warm water, a non-abrasive sponge, and a few drops of dish soap. Baking soda paste can also be used to eliminate any stains. Do not use vinegar or any harsh chemicals on copper sinks. Copper wax is also available for purchase in home stores and can be useful in maintaining a copper sink.

Tip ☆

To help preserve a copper sink, purchase a sink grid or mat to prevent dishes from directly coming into contact with the copper.

Step Two:

Cleaning a garbage disposal is quick and easy. The baking soda and vinegar combination will eliminate germs and any stubborn food particles hanging around. To clean a garbage disposal, turn it on and pour one cup (180 grams) of baking soda followed by one cup (237 mL) of distilled white vinegar. After the cycle ends, allow cool water to run for 30 seconds before turning off the garbage disposal. Toss a few handfuls of ice into the garbage disposal while the eater is running to finish the cleaning process. The ice encourages any stuck particles to be disposed of while sharpening the garbage disposal blades.

If you'd like to take it a step further, cut a medium-sized lemon into slices and allow the garbage disposal to grind them up. The lemon will deodorize any smells and the process takes under a minute.

Tip ☆

When using the garbage disposal function, be sure to run cold water. Hot water promotes the growth of bacterial while cold water will decrease the likelihood of odor.

Kitchenware and Utensils

Step One: Pots and Pans

If your dishes are clean and put away, you could argue this step isn't necessary, but a true deep cleaning should include kitchenware. Taking care of kitchenware is important if you want your tools to last. Plus, having extra clean pots, pans, and utensils is the cherry on top of a pristine kitchen.

Start by sorting out any cast iron pans. Depending on how often you use a cast iron. you may just have one or two pots/skillets in this category. Cast iron pans are great to use because over time they start to work better and better. When cast iron is cared for properly, these tools can be passed down, thrifted, or used year after year. Unlike other pans, cast iron skillets can and should be washed immediately even when they are hot. To keep them in great shape, try not to let food dry or crust onto them. Cast iron shouldn't be washed with soap or put into the dishwasher. However, conditioning cast iron pots and pans should definitely be done every once in a while. Conditioning cast iron is not hard and should be done every time the kitchen needs a deep cleaning. First, examine the pot or skillet and determine if any cleaning is needed. If any grime or crusted material is seen, throw water into the cast iron and bring it to a boil. This should get rid of the debris and scrubbing isn't necessary. Once the pan is cooled enough to touch, dry the cast iron right away using a microfiber towel or cloth. Cast iron should never be left to air dry. Next, to condition the cast iron, preheat the oven to 400 degrees Fahrenheit (205 degrees Celsius) and rub vegetable oil on the interior and exterior of the pan. Allow the pan to bake in the oven for at least one hour. This will ensure the no-stick aspect of the pan remains intact and will protect the cast iron.

Now inspect any ceramic pans you have. If any look dull, stained, or greasy, set them aside for cleaning. Fill each pan or pot one by one with water and place them on the stovetop. Bring water to a boil and add 1 cup (237 mL) of white vinegar. Boil for an additional five minutes and then turn off the heat. Then, add a few drops of dish soap. After one minute, use a mesh scrubber and any grime should come off with ease! Dry the pan and rub a dollop of vegetable oil on the surface. The vegetable oil conditions the pans and prevents grease from building up.

Step Two: Polish Utensils

Although you may not eat off of silver utensils every day, it's useful to know how to properly care for them. Polishing silver shouldn't take long and you likely already have the items needed. First, take a large, glass baking dish or aluminum baking pan and add one tablespoon (14.5 grams) of baking soda. Now add in one tablespoon (17 grams) of sea salt. Now add half a cup (118 mL) of white vinegar and stir. Add in one cup (237 mL) of boiling, hot water and stir before adding the silver utensils. Each utensil should be submerged in the mixture for 30 seconds or up to five minutes, depending on how tarnished the utensils are. Dry the utensils using a microfiber cloth before storing.

Clean Out the Drawers

Step One:

Chances are you already have some type of storage unit for organizing silverware and utensils. Check to see if the storage unit is dishwasher safe and remove the contents of the drawer. Wipe down each drawer and place the organizer back into the drawer after it is clean. Follow the same steps for each drawer. Not only is this important to eliminate germs, but also to prevent insects. This step is also an excellent time to go through your belongings in the kitchen and throw away/donate anything not being used.

The Refrigerator

Step One:

Unfortunately, this is a task many push off and don't enjoy. However, with these simple steps, cleaning the refrigerator can be done with ease! Even when being careful, small spills and drops of food inevitably line the refrigerator. What's worse is that the tiniest spills can sit for weeks and give off terrible odors. Unfortunately, the refrigerator can harbor a lot of germs and bacteria that you definitely don't want getting into food! When cleaning out the refrigerator, it's best to do so with natural cleaners as you don't want to expose any food to chemicals.

The first step is to remove everything from the refrigerator. Check each item and consider how old the item is. You will find that many items are ready to be discarded or have expired. This is also an excellent time to check condiments and their expiration dates, so that expired food isn't accidentally consumed. Make a list of items to repurchase if you find yourself throwing away popular items.

Tip ☆

Plan to clean the refrigerator right before a big grocery shop. Not only will this save time when removing the contents in the refrigerator, but it will limit the time the food spends outside of the refrigerator, preventing any spoiling.

Step Two:

Starting from the top, start to remove any shelving or drawers possible and place them on the counter near the sink. Wipe down the bottom, top, sides, and door of the fridge using a dish soap and sponge. Use the sponge to soak up all the soap and use a damp paper towel to make sure no soap or grime is left behind. Use a towel or microfiber cloth to ensure everything in the refrigerator is dry. Depending on how long this part takes, return any products to the refrigerator that tend to spoil quickly.

Use the same technique to wash any removed drawers and dry completely before returning them to the refrigerator. This whole process should only take 15 to 20 minutes.

Step Three:

If you own a stainless steel refrigerator, clean the outside by spraying white vinegar onto a microfiber cloth. Always rub in the same direction as the grain. Afterwards, dab a small amount of olive oil onto a paper towel and rub onto the steel to polish. If your refrigerator is not steel, the same can be accomplished by using a sponge or towel with dish soap or white vinegar.

The Freezer

Step One:

Luckily, the freezer is an appliance that only needs to be cleaned thoroughly once a year. Spot cleaning any small messes is usually sufficient throughout the year, but once a year it's good to clean the whole freezer.

To start, disconnect or unplug the freezer from the power source. Remove the food from the freezer and discard any freezer-burnt or spoiled food. Store the food in a second freezer or in a cooler filled with ice.

Step Two:

Defrost the freezer by turning on the defrost setting, naturally, or place a boil of hot water in the freezer and close the door. Note that some freezers are frost-free and it's best to check with the freezer's manual for this step. Do not chip away at ice or frost as this can ruin the freezer.

Step Three:

While the freezer is defrosting, check the coils usually located in the back of the freezer. Use a vacuum or cloth to remove any dust or debris. This will allow the freezer to run properly and more efficiently.

Step Four:

Remove any shelving or drawers and wash them with dish soap in the sink. Use baking soda and water to scrub the freezer after the freezer is completely frost-free. Be sure to rinse the freezer with water to ensure no residue is left over and dry completely using a clean towel. Turn the freezer back on and wait 20 to 30 minutes before placing the food back inside.

Pantry

Step One:

Start by looking at each shelf in the pantry from an organizational standpoint. Is everything grouped together in categories that make sense? If not, not to worry because doing so won't take a lot of additional effort.

The first step to cleaning a pantry is to remove all the items. However, when doing so, try to group things together that make sense. For example, start by removing any baking goods and put them on one section of the counter while you clean the pantry. Then remove all snacks and group them together. Continue removing every item from the pantry and grouping them on the counter until no items remain. Throw out any expired items and items that are never used.

Step Two:

Take a look at the pantry and you may notice that some areas appear dirtier than others. For instance, sugar, oil, and flour often leave traces behind. Take mental notes of what is causing your pantry to become dirty and save them for later.

Now that everything is removed, look at the material of the shelves to assess how to properly clean them. If they're wooden, you may need to use a different cleaner. Take a vacuum cleaner and use the hose to vacuum each shelf. You can also use a cloth but a vacuum is the easiest way to get all the crumbs and to be sure they are not getting pushed around or onto the floor. After vacuuming the surface, the shelves should be quite clean.

Step Three:

Unless you have wooden shelves, prepare a solution using one part white vinegar and one part water. Add in any favorite essential oils like lemon, orange, mint, or wood aromas. If scrubbing is required, sprinkle baking soda onto the surface first before spraying the vinegar mixture. The vinegar will disinfect the surfaces and eliminate any germs.

Now that the surfaces are clean, dry them off before returning any items. Use a microfiber towel to collect any dust that wasn't picked up by the vacuum. Remember to return the items in groups. And for the items that leave behind residue on the shelves, place a plate or newspaper under the items. Oil, sugar, and flour are likely the main culprits and placing a plate or newspaper underneath them will ensure a quicker clean the next time around.

Garbage Can

Step One:

A deep cleaning is the perfect opportunity to clean out the garbage can. Whether you own a garbage can or trash bin, the bottom and sides of the container likely have bacteria. Cleaning a trash bin is simple and will prevent and eliminate unwanted odors.

Start by emptying the trash bin or container. Plan to clean the garbage can after the bag is full, so a new bag can be placed in the garbage can afterwards. If you're able to do the next steps outside, it may be easier.

Step Two:

Combine warm water and dish soap in a spray bottle or use a soapy rag to wipe down the entire garbage can including the outside, top, and bottom of the can. Sprinkle baking soda all over in the interior of the can and allow the can to sit for 15 to 20 minutes. Next, use a sponge and scrub the can. Afterwards, use a hose to rinse the can and allow the can to dry outside if possible. A clean towel can also be used if doing this inside.

Tip ☆

Throw magazine or newspaper pages into the bottom of the garbage can before putting a new, clean bag in the can. This will catch and absorb any liquids and allows for easy removal every time you empty the trash can. Another trick is to sprinkle baking soda into the trash can after food goes in. This isn't a necessary step everytime something is discarded but the baking soda will prevent odors after large amounts of foods go into the bin.

Countertops and Backsplash

Step One:

How you clean your countertop will depend on what type of material the countertop is made from. Usually, countertops are made from different types of stones. Cleaning an area of the countertop is usually a daily task, but during a deep cleaning, it's a good idea to clean the entire countertop to get rid of any germs or crumbs.

Tip ☆

Always clean the kitchen top to bottom. Wiping down appliances and countertops will probably lead to some crumbs dropping to the floor. Cleaning the kitchen top to bottom will save you a lot of time and effort and you'll only have to clean a surface once. Always vacuum and mop the floors last.

Granite countertops are made of a hard material and are less porous than other stones. Regardless, almost all granite countertops are sealed with a solution that protects them. To check if your granite countertop is sealed, drop a few drops of water onto the surface. If the water beads up, the seal is performing properly and you're good to go. If not, or if the water absorbs into the counter, you may want to look into getting the counter sealed again. If water can absorb into the counter, it's likely other food or oil is damaging the countertop.

To clean granite countertops, never use harsh chemicals unless they say they are granite safe. Truthfully, granite countertops can be properly washed with a bit of dish soap and a microfiber cloth. A microfiber cloth will exfoliate gently and won't leave streaks. If you're countertops are really dirty or have anything stuck to them, add a small amount of rubbing alcohol to the soapy mixture.

Unlike granite, marble is a porous material and will absorb oil and colors if not taken care of properly. Be sure that your countertop is sealed and check with the manufacturer on how often the counter should receive sealant.

To remove stains from marble, cornstarch will come in handy. In a small bowl, mix cornstarch with a few drops of water to create a thick milk-like consistency. Apply the mixture to any grease or stains and allow the paste to sit on the counter for up to 24 hours, if necessary. Use a sponge to wipe off the mixture.

Cleaning marble countertops is easy. Use a few drops of milk dish soap and a kitchen sponge. Use the scrubbing side if necessary. If any spills or crumbs are stuck to the surface, allow the soapy water to sit on the countertops for a few minutes to avoid harsh scrubbing. Be sure to dry the countertop after cleaning.

Tip ☆

On a marble countertop, the appearance of scratches can be minimized by using a little baking soda. Pour baking soda over the scratch and rub a damp kitchen sponge over the scratch. Use up and down motions before rinsing and drying the area. The scratch should be visibly diminished.

For laminate or quartz countertops, use one part water and one part vinegar to clean and sanitize the countertops.

Kitchen Table and Chairs

Step One:

Kitchen chairs are often overlooked when it comes to cleaning the kitchen, but they shouldn't be. Like other parts of the kitchen, kitchen chairs are not immune to spills and crumbs. Overtime, chairs can get worn out depending on how much use they receive. Maintaining kitchen chairs will depend on the type owned. Many kitchen chairs have some type of cushion to make sitting more comfortable while others will be easy to clean with a little solution.

To clean upholstered kitchen chairs, start by using the hose of a vacuum to go over each cushion. This will eliminate any surface crumbs but may also draw out any dirt or dust in the cushion. Second, gather baking soda and vinegar. Use baking soda first and sprinkle a generous amount over the chair. Use your fingers, a toothbrush, or a gentle brush to lightly exfoliate the chair. This step removes any dirt or grime on the surface.

In a spray bottle, mix one part vinegar and one part warm water adding a few drops of dish detergent. Give the spray bottle a shake and spray the mixture over the chairs. Be sure to spray an even amount over the entire surface to avoid any water marks. Use a cloth to rub the mixture into the seat. The detergent will dissolve any grease stains and the vinegar will get rid of any germs. Allow the chairs to dry outside or place a fan in the kitchen for good ventilation.

For any hard stains, mix half a cup (118 mL) of dish soap and one cup (237 mL) of hydrogen peroxide in a glass spray bottle. Spray the mixture onto the stain and let the chair sit for a minute or two before giving it a gentle scrub. You may want to color test this procedure in an unsuspicious area before spraying onto a noticeable spot.

For wooden chairs, a similar mixture of one part water and one part vinegar can be used. Afterwards, be sure to dry the chair completely as it's not good to let water sit on wood. To polish and restore wood, add a few drops of olive oil to a microfiber cloth and rub the oil over the chair. This whole process is super easy and your chairs will look good as new! This same process can be used on other chairs too like plastic or laminate.

Step Two:

Kitchen tables usually receive a cleaning on a frequent basis, but take this time to really inspect the table and give it a good clean. Keeping the kitchen table clean is important to prevent germs and bacteria from spreading. Depending on the type of kitchen table owned, follow the same steps as above to clean, disinfect, and polish the kitchen table.

Sweep, Vacuum, and Mop

Step One:

Start by vacuuming or sweeping the kitchen as best as possible. If you are a pet owner, a vacuum may work better to collect hair. Use the hose on the vacuum to get every corner and inch of the kitchen. Be on the lookout for any cobwebs and be sure to remove them with the vacuum. Although sweeping and vacuuming is quite self-explanatory, there are a few tips and tricks to know.

Be sure to sanitize the dust pan frequently. Because germs, particles, and hair is swept into the dust pan, germs and bacteria are ever present. Use a disinfectant wipe, dish soap, or rubbing alcohol after a few uses.

To remove dust bunnies from the broom, gather a hot glue gun and a wide tooth comb. Glue the comb horizontally near the handle with the bristles pointing upwards. Now, when sweeping, drag the broom across the comb to remove any dust bunnies.

Just how the dust pan can collect germs, the broom can as well. Cleaning and replacing brooms are necessary to avoid spreading germs throughout the house. Clean the broom after three or four heavy uses or when the bottom bristles look dirty. To clean the broom, place hot water, dish soap, or vinegar in a large bucket. Allow the broom to soak for at least thirty minutes. After thirty minutes, remove the broom and rinse with hot water. Leave the broom outside or point upwards to dry.

Step Two:

To clean the floors, white vinegar can be a great, inexpensive solution. Vinegar is safe for linoleum, tile, vinyl, and wood floors. Vinegar is also non-toxic and eco-friendly, making it a great choice. In a bucket, combine half a cup (118 mL) of vinegar and 1 gallon (3.8 L) of hot water. Mop the floor one section at a time, dipping the mop in the vinegar solution frequently. Use scrubbing motions as needed. Vinegar is great on kitchen floors because extra rinsing is not needed which cuts the time spent mopping in half.

Examine the floors after they are dry and decide if the grout needs extra cleaning. This may not apply to some depending on the type of floor you have. Grout can be cleaned with only boiling hot water and a metal bristle brush. Although tile steamers and chemicals are available to purchase, hot water and a metal bristle brush works just as well, if not better.

Tip ☆

Invest in a swifter like item and use a reusable microfiber pad to clean the floor in between washes. The same effect can be done by dampening a microfiber cloth and securing it to a broom using rubber bands. Wearing socks and slippers can also lessen the germs and dirt spread throughout the house.

Kitchen Checklist

Dusting

1. Dust or clean the top of the cabinets using cloth or solution. Place newspaper, magazine pages, or wax paper on top of the cabinets.
2. Dust the top of the refrigerator. Use the same solution to wipe down the sides and front of the refrigerator.
3. Wipe down window sills using a dust solution.

Cabinets

1. Wipe the outside of the cabinets.
2. Remove items from the cabinets and wipe down the inside of the cabinets.
4. Clean the cabinet handles with disinfectant. Continue to clean other handles on the refrigerator, freezer, microwave, knobs, etc.

Appliances

1. Clean the microwave using a measuring cup filled with water and lemon. Wipe down the outside of the microwave.
2. Clean the stove top.
3. Clean the inside of the oven.
4. Clean the glass window on the door of the oven.
5. Soak and clean oven racks overnight.
6. Clean the spray arm of the dishwasher.
7. Do a vinegar cycle through the dishwasher.
5. Sprinkle baking soda on the bottom of the dishwasher and do a complete cycle.

Sink and Garbage Disposal

1. Scrub the sink.

2. Deodorize and clean the garbage disposal.

Kitchenware and Utensils

1. Clean cast iron pots, pans, and skillets.
2. Clean ceramic pots, pans, and skillets.
3. Polish silverware.

Clean Out the Drawers

1. Clean the bottom and sides of drawers. Donate or throw away anything not being used.

Refrigerator

1. Empty the contents of the refrigerator. Throw away any expired items.
2. Remove any possible shelving or drawers and wash.
3. Clean the interior of the refrigerator by wiping the bottom, sides, and top.
4. Clean the exterior of the refrigerator.

Freezer

1. Disconnect the freezer from the power source.
2. Remove food and place into backup freezer or cooler filled with ice.
3. Defrost freezer using one of the methods above or with the directions in the freezer's manual.
4. Remove shelving or racks and clean once the freezer is defrosted.
5. Wipe out the freezer and clean.
6. Use a towel to dry the freezer before turning it back on. Place the food back into the freezer after 30 minutes.

Pantry

1. Remove items from the pantry and place them into groups

that make sense. For example, snacks, oils, and baking materials should all be placed together.

2. Discard any expired or unused items.
3. Clean the shelves using the method above.
4. Return the items in groups and place newspaper or a plate under items that make messes.

Garbage Bin

1. Remove any trash or the trash bag.
2. Apply dish soap and baking soda to every part of the can. Leave the can to soak for 20 minutes. (Clean the can outside if possible.)
3. Scrub the can using a sponge and use a garden hose to rinse. Allow the can to dry outside or use a clean towel.
4. Place newspaper or baking soda at the bottom of the can.

Countertops

1. Wash and wipe down countertops using a method above. Determine the material of your countertop before proceeding.

Kitchen Table and Chairs

1. Wipe down kitchen chairs and upholstery.
2. Wipe down kitchen table.

Sweep, Vacuum, and Mop

1. Clean the kitchen floors by sweeping or vacuuming.
2. Mop the kitchen floors using a vinegar solution.
3. Clean tile grout if necessary.

Living Spaces

Living rooms, dens, and common spaces typically endure a lot of wear and tear due to the high traffic they receive from family and guests. Usually, the cleanliness of these spaces is the most important out of any other room in the house. Having a clean living room can really set the mood for the entire house. This section will go through how to clean common items found in these spaces and give tips and tricks to keeping them clean!

Pick Up Things That Don't Belong

Many times, unnecessary clutter is what dictates a room unclean. In the living room, this could mean dishes, items of clothing, backpacks, or garbage. Start by looking around the room and placing items in their proper place. Try to put items in their correct spots, clean dishes left in the living room, and collect trash.

Clean Furniture or Upholstery

Cleaning furniture is an important part of a deep cleaning. You may not realize it but over time, furniture is bound to get a little dirty. To keep the living room clean, you can make a few house rules like no shoes or food, but for practicality, not every family wishes to do so. Either way, cleaning furniture is always a good idea once in awhile to get rid of germs, dander, or bacteria.

<u>Step One</u>:

Start by using a vacuum hose over the furniture. Not only will this collect anything on the surface but it will also draw any dust or dirt upwards and allow a deeper clean in the next step.

<u>Step Two:</u>

To clean leather furniture, prepare the following recipe in a spray bottle. It may be a good idea to test the mixture on a small, unseen area of the leather first to see how it will react. However, this mixture is perfect for almost all leather furniture.

- ½ cup (118 mL) white vinegar
- ¼ cup (54 grams) coconut oil
- ½ teaspoon (7 mL) dish soap
- 10 drops essential oil (orange, lemon, clove, etc.)

Give the bottle a good shake and spray the mixture onto a microfiber cloth. Try not to use anything too harsh as you don't want to damage the leather. After a few minutes of rubbing and scrubbing, your leather will be clean and conditioned.

To clean upholstery or fabric, use a combination of:

- ½ cup (118 mL) rubbing alcohol
- ½ cup (118 mL) vinegar
- 5 drops essential oil of choice

Mix the above ingredients in a spray bottle and use a gentle brush, towel, or sponge to go over furniture. The essential oils are optional but will leave a more pleasant odor.

Disinfect

Because the living room has a lot of commonly used items, it's a good idea to disinfect items touched by the whole household. This is an easy step and should be done frequently, not just during a deep cleaning.

Items that you'll want to use a disinfectant on are any door handles, all television remotes, game controllers, and buttons on the TV and game consoles. Be sure to look around and find other items commonly touched. During the cold and flu season, be sure to disinfect those items frequently.

If you don't own a disinfectant or prefer a natural one, use a bit of white vinegar or rubbing alcohol. Essential oils are a great resource that produce a nice aroma.

Now is a great time to wipe the television screen. This can be done with a microfiber cloth and a little warm water. Harsh chemicals should not be used on a TV screen but a damp, soapy rag can be used if necessary.

Dusting

Take some time now to dust the living room. During a deep clean, it's best to dust as many areas as possible, even the ones you may not usually dust. Look high, and start by dusting the highest points of the room, then work your way down. Hard to reach areas and corners may benefit from using a vacuum to dust instead. Don't forget to dust books, coffee tables, end tables, the ceiling fan, picture frames, windows sils, blinds, the back of the television, and above shelves! Plants can also collect dust. To dust plants, use a hair dryer on low heat. Although the dust won't be collected, it will fall to the floor and will be picked up when vacuuming.

Tip ☆

To dust the ceiling fan, use an old pillow case and insert the fan blade into the middle. Secure the pillow case around the fan and pull. The pillow case should collect the dust and will prevent it from falling.

To dust the blinds on a window, start by lowering them as far down as possible. Open them enough to create a horizontal surface. Using kitchen tongs, secure a microfiber cloth on each tong using rubber bands. By using this technique, you should be able to go over each blind with ease, using a left to right motion or vice versa.

Curtains, Pillows, and Blankets

<u>Step One</u>:

Many don't realize that not only do curtains collect dust, they also collect debris and particles when the window is open. When curtains aren't maintained, much of this dust or dirt spreads into the home. Maintaining and cleaning them regularly will improve the air quality of your home and will help with any allergy symptoms.

How you clean your curtains will depend on the type owned. For starters, take the curtains down and remove any hardware. Take the curtains outside and give them a good shake. You should see a lot of dust and particles flying off of them.

If you have a garment or fabric curtains, place them in the wash and wash them using cold water or on a delicate cycle. You can add a small amount of detergent but you'll want to make sure the detergent won't stain the curtains. Dry the curtains on the lowest heat setting or in a well ventilated area. Only wash one or two curtains at a time to prevent damaging them.

For lace or sheer fabric curtains, after shaking them out outside, place them in a bathtub filled with cold water. Only wash one panel at a time. A small amount of dish detergent can be used but don't overdo it. Place the panel into the soapy water and allow them to soak for 5 to 10 minutes. Afterwards, give the water a little swirl and shake away any visible debris. Drain the soapy water and fill the tub again with plain cold water to rinse the panel. Dry the panel in a well ventilated area. Repeat this process as needed.

<u>Step Two</u>:

Washing decorative pillows should be done every so often to keep them clean and in good condition. This step shouldn't require much effort as most pillows are made of washable material.

Check each pillow in the living area and see if the cover can be removed. If so, remove the cover and turn it inside out. This will protect the decorative aspects of the pillow when being washed. Place the cover in the washing machine and wash on a cold or delicate cycle. Detergent can be used but be sure it's gentle and advertised as safe for fabrics. Dry the cover outside or hang-dry if possible. The no heat setting on the dryer can also be used. Every once in a while, wash the pillow itself using the same technique. If your pillow doesn't have a removable case or is made of wool, velvet, silk, feathers, or upholstery, it's probably best to have them dry cleaned.

Step Three:

Gather blankets commonly used and place in the washer on a delicate, cold cycle. Afterwards, dry the blanket on a low heat setting or in a well ventilated space.

Vacuum, Sweep, or Mop

To finish up cleaning the living room, vacuum or mop the floors. Deep cleaning the living room likely pushed dirt and dust to the floor so this step should always be last to ensure everything gets picked up. This is also the time to use your carpet cleaner if you have one or invest in professional help. Over time, carpets get dirty and collects everything floating around the house. You should clean your carpets up to twice annually.

Living Room Checklist

Return Items to Proper Room

1. Collect any items that don't belong in the living room and return them to their correct place. Collect trash, clean leftover dishes, or put clothing in the laundry basket.

Furniture

1. Use a vacuum hose on furniture to collect everything on the surface.
2. Spot clean or deep clean furniture to get rid of any germs and dander using a method above.

Disinfect

1. Disinfect door handles, television remotes, buttons, game controllers, and other frequently touched items.
2. Wipe and clean the television screen.

Dusting

1. Find and remove any cobwebs. Dust the entire room. Start from the top and look for any horizontal surface that could collect dust. Areas should include but aren't limited to the tops of books/magazines, coffee tables, end tables, the ceiling fan, picture frames, windows sils, blinds, the back of the television, and above/in between shelving.

Curtains, Pillows, and Blankets

1. Remove each curtain and shake outside.
2. Wash curtains using a method above.
3. Wash each pillow or spot clean stains.
4. Gather and wash blankets.

Floors

1. Sweep, vaccum, or mop the floors to ensure no dirt or dust is left. Use a carpet cleaner if owned or consider enlisting professional help.

The Office

Although you may not have an entire room dedicated to an office, these tips can still be helpful. This section can also be helpful for any place where bills, schoolwork, reading, or studying is done. These tips can also apply to a workspace in an office outside of your home. This section might be a little different for everyone, but keeping a clean, germ-free space is important to most. At this point, some of these tasks have already become familiar, so just important notes will be discussed.

Dusting

Like any other room, start by dusting. Because dust particles like to float around, it's best to do this step first. Start to dust above cabinets and on the tops of any furniture. This can be done using a vacuum cleaner for hard to reach spots and a damp microfiber cloth. If your space has a lot of books, don't be afraid to vacuum off the tops, as most will be filled with dust.

Tip ☆

To remove dust from lamp shades, use a lint roller. The stickiness will pick up the debris without pushing it further into the lamp or spreading the dust into the air.

Disinfect

Whether you have a home office or not, keeping your work space germ-free will help ward off any illnesses. Use disinfectant wipes or a little white vinegar and wipe down commonly touched items almost daily. In an office, these surfaces will include a desk chair, pens or pencils, doorknobs, keyboards, touchscreens, mouse, cabinet drawers, files, and the printer.

Although disinfecting wipes are available for purchase, you can make your own using inexpensive and natural ingredients. Being frequently exposed to chemicals isn't good for your health and these wipes leave an aroma that can be customizable. These wipes are perfect for the house or to bring to the office. To maintain a germ-free environment, each morning before working, use one wipe to disinfect the space around you. All you will need is:

- 2 cups (500 mL) warm water
- 1 cup (237 mL) rubbing alcohol
- A few drops of dish soap
- One paper towel roll
- Glass container (to fit paper towel roll if possible)
- A few drops of essential oils (lemon, orange, etc.)

The container used should tightly fit the paper towels and be a cylinder shape. If this is not possible, tear each paper towel into sheets and use a square or rectangle container to fit the paper towels. Mix the wet ingredients in a bowl and pour the mixture over the paper towels. After the paper towels are soaked, the cardboard cylinder in the middle of the roll should be removed so the towel sheets are easier to tear off when needed.

Tip ☆

To reach hard to get crumbs, dust, and particles, take the sticky part of a sticky note and run it through the gaps of a keyboard. Depending on how dirty the keyboard is, you may need more than one sticky note, but this is a quick, foolproof tip to really get the keyboard clean.

Floors

Untangle any cords lying around on the floor. Also, look down to the floors. If you spot any dust or crumbs, vacuum or mop the floors for the final touch!

Office Checklist

Dusting

1. Dust furniture.
2. Use a wood cleaner on furniture and desks.
3. Dust the windows and blinds.
4. Use a lint roller on lamp shades to remove dust.
5. Use a vacuum to go over furniture and eliminate dust.

Disinfect

1. Wipe down keyboard, computer, and mouse with disinfectant.
2. Disinfect handles, light switches, knobs, and commonly touched items.
3. Wipe the inside of drawers.
4. Clean windows and mirrors.
5. Wipe down the walls and eliminate cobwebs.

Floors

1. Untangle cords.
2. Vacuum or mop the floors.

Bathroom Cleaning

Whether you like to entertain or not, the state of a bathroom always leaves an impression. If you live alone, your bathroom may need less frequent cleaning but if you live with a spouse and kids, it quickly becomes evident how often the bathroom needs cleaning. Unlike other rooms, bathrooms or powder rooms come in a higher quantity throughout the house. The bathrooms used the most should always be cleaned on a frequent basis, whereas others may just need a bit of spot cleaning. A deep cleaning is a great opportunity to get each bathroom pristine so you don't have to spend as much time each time you clean it.

The Shower

Step One: Shower Walls and Floors

Start by removing all items from the shower so you have an empty space to work in. Be sure to discard anything that's empty or unused. If you're able to remove the shower head, do so and spray the walls with hot water. A cup can also be used to achieve the same effect. Try to rid as much hair and dirt off the walls before getting started with the next steps.

In a spray bottle, add warm vinegar and a few drops of dish soap. Give the bottle a shake and spray the mixture all over the shower walls and floor. Let the solution sit on the walls for 30 minutes. The vinegar works to remove stains, kill germs, and neutralize any odors. The dish soap will help eliminate any grease or grime stuck to the walls from dirt or soap. After 30 minutes, use a scrubbing brush to go over each wall before giving the shower a good rinse. This solution is safe on vinyl and tile walls.

Step Two: Shower Head

The shower head is often neglected when cleaning the bathroom.

Water usually contains trace minerals, like calcium. When water sits in the shower or on the shower head, a buildup usually occurs. Cleaning the shower head is easy and only needs to be done during a deep clean or every couple of months.

To clean a shower head, all you will need is white vinegar, a large ziplock bag, and a rubber band. First, fill the plastic bag with about 1 cup (237 mL) of white vinegar. Use more if needed. Place the ziplock around the shower head and secure it with a rubber band. Position the shower head horizontally so the entire head is in contact with the vinegar. Allow the shower head to soak for at least one hour. Afterwards, use a toothbrush to remove any scum or calcium left behind, which at this point should be falling right off.

Step Three: Shower Drain

The shower drain can often get clogged and it can be a headache when this happens. Hair, particles, and debris can get trapped and prevent water from draining properly. Luckily, the shower drain can be unclogged and cleaned easily.

First, remove the cap from the drain. To clean the drain you will need baking soda, vinegar, and a metal hook. A metal hook can be made by simply taking a metal hanger and twisting it into a long hook or tool. Once you have your metal hook, put it into the drain and begin twisting until you're able to feel the gunk attaching to the wire. Using a twist and pull motion, try to remove as much from the drain as possible.

After removing debris from the drain, pour a generous amount of baking soda down the drain. Follow this up by pouring a cup (237 mL) of white vinegar down the drain. You will notice a chemical reaction taking place and a white, foaming substance. Leave the mixture to sit for about 10 minutes and then let the hot water run down the drain for one minute.

Tip ☆

Every few weeks, pour baking soda and boiling hot water down the drain to kill bacterial and fight clogging. If your shower is well maintained, this step may be preferred over the metal hook instructions. To prevent the shower from clogging, never pour dirty water from mopping or other activities in the shower or bath. Always discard outside (if water is chemical-free) or into the toilet for disposal.

Step Four: Curtain or Door

The curtain or door of the shower is usually one of the first things to get dirty, or need replacement. Most of time time, soap and grime is splashed onto the door/curtain and isn't able to be properly rinsed like other parts of the shower. Minerals from the water or debris have a way of building up on the door or curtain and making them look dirty.

To clean a plastic shower curtain, place the curtain in the washing machine with two or three full sized towels. The towels will protect the curtain liner and the washing machine. If there is any mold or mildew on the curtain, add one cup (180 grams) of baking soda to the washer drum. The baking soda will act as an exfoliate and minimize the appearance of mold or mildew. Run a hot water cycle using a dab of regular laundry detergent and use the delicate setting if possible. To dry the curtain, simple hang it back up in the shower. Open a window or use a fan in the bathroom, if possible, until the curtain is dry. If you do not own a washing machine or wish to just spot clean the liner, use a rag with baking soda and scrub the areas that need attention.

Tip ☆

To prevent mildew and mold from growing on the shower curtain, always close the curtain. This allows better drying and prevents moisture from getting trapped in the curtain. Turn on the fan or leave a window open if possible after showering to help get the added moisture out of the air.

For more delicate curtains or curtains made of fabric, you may wish to opt out of using a washing machine. A similar result can be achieved by filling the bathtub one third of the way with warm water, adding in a few drops of laundry detergent, and a cup (237 mL) of vinegar. Let the curtain soak in the water for 20 to 30 minutes before rinsing. A toothbrush can be used to scrub areas that need a little extra attention.

Step Five: Shower Door

To remove water stains and grime from a glass shower door, mix one part of white vinegar (warm) and one part dawn dish soap. Mix the two in a glass bottle and spray both sides of the glass door. Allow the mixture to sit on the glass for five minutes or clean with a sponge right away depending on how dirty the door is. Dry the door with a microfiber cloth and enjoy a streak-free, clean shower door!

The Toilet

Step One:

The toilet is usually everyone's least favorite to clean. However, by using the mixture below, the whole process will be done extremely quick and the toilet will be good as new. Prepare the following in a spray bottle:

- ½ cup (90 grams) baking soda
- ½ teaspoon (3 grams) tea tree oil
- 1 cup (237 mL) white vinegar
- A few drops of essential oil (orange, lemon, etc.)

Spray the mixture on the exterior and interior of the toilet and let the solution sit for 10 minutes. Don't forget the base of the toilet and the areas immediately surrounding. The handle and lid of the toilet should also be sprayed with the solution. Take a sponge or microfiber cloth to wipe off the cleaner after allowing it to soak. Finish by sprinkling baking soda inside the bowl and using a toilet brush to exfoliate away any grime. Flush the toilet for the final step.

Step Two:

The toilet tank can often host bacteria and germs unknowingly. During a deep cleaning, it's best to give the tank a little attention to thoroughly clean the toilet. When cleaning the tank, be mindful of the chains and parts inside. You'll want to avoid them so the toilet doesn't break or get ruined. Pour two cups of vinegar (500 mL) into the tank and let it sit for an hour. Do not use the toilet at this time. After an hour, put on gloves and give the walls and parts a gentle rub using a toothbrush or a sponge. To finish, rinse everything by simply flushing the toilet.

The Sink, Faucet, and Countertops

Step One:

Although the sink may look clean, it's not immune to germs and bacteria. The sink often catches hair, debris, toothpaste, and hairspray. To clean the sink, use dish soap and a sponge to gently exfoliate the grime away. White vinegar can also be used to get rid of any germs. Use a microfiber cloth afterwards to dry the sink.

Step Two:

Because faucets are often used and touched frequently, it's likely they'll become dirty quickly. During a deep clean, take the cleaning a step further by doing a vinegar soak on the faucet. Not only will this eliminate germs, but most stains as well. Using a spray bottle, drench toilet paper or paper towel in vinegar. Wrap the soaked towels around the faucet and back of the sink where watermarks or stains appear. Let the paper towels or toilet paper sit for one hour.

Rinse the area with water and use a microfiber cloth to dry the area. This trick requires little to no effort and will save you time trying to scrub out difficult rust or stains. To restore the shine to the faucet and handles, dab a generous amount of baby oil on a cotton pad and wipe the appliances.

Step Three:

Cleaning the countertops only requires a sponge and a little dish soap. Be sure to give the counter a good rinse with water before drying with a microfiber cloth.

Mirror, Trash Can, Rugs, and Bath Mats

Step One:

A dirty mirror can make a seemingly clean bathroom look dirty. A clean mirror will set the tone and give off an overall clean feel. To clean the mirror, use a glass cleaner or a paper towel with vinegar. Dry the mirror with a microfiber towel to avoid streaks.

Step Two:

Empty and remove any trash in the bathroom. Take it a step further by wiping down the trash bin with dish soap and a sponge. Vinegar can also be used to kill any germs. Sprinkle a bit of baking soda in the bottom before putting in a new bag to lessen any odors.

Step Three:

Take any rugs or bath mats and shake them outside. Then, wash them on a cold, delicate cycle in the washing machine. Check the tags of the rugs to see if they have any special instructions. Dry the rugs or mats outside, or hang them in a well ventilated area to dry. If you do not have a washer, the mats and rugs can be washed in the bathtub by using a little detergent and warm water. Allow them to soak before rinsing with cold water and drying. Replace any hand towels with new ones.

The Vent and Floors

Step One:

The vent of a bathroom often collects dust and debris. Before cleaning the floors, safely use a ladder if needed to clean the vent. A vacuum can come in handy for this part and will remove most of the dust. After using the vacuum, use a rag with vinegar to further kill any germs and clean.

Step Two:

Clean the bathroom floors by first vacuuming or sweeping them. Then use the solution of your choice to eliminate dirt and kill any bacteria.

Tip ☆

For those who can't seem to get rid of urine odors, apply shaving cream around the toilet area. Even a budget-friendly shaving cream will do the trick so there is no need to buy anything expensive. Apply a generous amount around the toilet and base of the floors and leave the cream to sit for a few hours. Overnight soaking may be needed depending on the odor issue. After a few hours, remove the shaving cream by using a towel or sponge and you'll be amazed at how the odor is completely gone.

Bathroom Checklist

The Shower

1. Spray or use a cup to get shower walls wet.
2. Prepare the solution above and coat shower walls. Allow the cleaner to soak on the walls for 30 minutes before rinsing.
3. Soak the shower head in white vinegar by placing 1 cup (237 mL) of white vinegar in a plastic bag and securing it to the showerhead with an elastic.
4. Soak for one hour and use a toothbrush to gently scrub the showerhead before rinsing.
5. Assemble a metal hook. This can be done by using a metal hanger.
6. Place the hook into the drain and using an upward, twisting motion, remove as much from the drain as possible.
7. Pour a generous amount of baking soda into the drain, followed by one cup (237 mL) of water. Leave the mixture for 10 minutes before rinsing it down with hot water.
8. Wash shower curtains or liners by using the methods above.
9. Clean the shower door using the solution above.

The Toilet

1. Clean the interior and exterior using the solution above. Don't forget the lid and handle of the toilet.
2. Wipe the base of the toilet.
3. Clean the toilet tank by using vinegar.

The Sink, Faucet, and Countertops

1. Clean the sink using a sponge and dish soap.
2. Do a vinegar soak on the faucet and sink areas.
3. Rub baby oil on the faucet to restore shine.
4. Clean the countertops using a sponge and a dab of dish soap. Dry with a microfiber cloth for a streak-free shine.

The Mirror, Trash Can, Rugs, and Bath Mats

1. Clean the mirror using a microfiber towel or paper towel and solution.
2. Empty trash bin.
3. Clean trash bin with dish soap and sponge. Dry.
4. Sprinkle baking soda at the bottom of the trash can to eliminate odors.
5. Shake bath mats and rugs outside.
6. Wash bath mats and rugs in the bathtub or in the washer on a cold, delicate setting. Allow heat-free drying.
7. Replace any hand towels with new, fresh clean ones.

The Vent and Floors

1. Clean the vent of the bathroom by taking a vacuum to the vent. This will collect any dust. Use a vinegar or disinfectant solution over the vent.
2. Vacuum or sweep the floors.
3. Mop the floors using your preferred solution.
4. Apply shaving cream around the toilet to get rid of any odors.

Bedroom Cleaning

The bedrooms of a house are extremely important for restful sleeping, relaxing, and rejuvenating. Having a clean bedroom will keep the mind clear and allow proper rest. Keeping a bedroom clean doesn't require a lot of hard work but busy times can often leave the bedroom looking like a mess. A deep cleaning in the bedroom should take place every couple of weeks to maintain a good environment for rejuvenation.

Dust and Disinfect

Step One:

Start by dusting and disinfecting everything possible. Remember to always start at the highest point so anything that falls can be collected later. The most common places that will need dusting are in the corners of the ceiling, on top of furniture, and lamp shades. A vacuum hose may come in handy to get hard to reach areas. Don't forget to dust the television, the back of the television, on top of books, candles, and the wardrobe. Around the windows and blinds are also places that frequently collect dust.

Tip ☆

To gently clean and remove dust from walls, take a microfiber cloth and secure it over a broom. The broom will allow you to get hard to reach high places and the microfiber cloth will collect dust.

Step Two:

To make sure everything is germ-free, you'll want to disinfect items and areas that are often touched. In the bedroom this includes door handles, light switches, remotes, the toilet handle, shower handle, and knobs on a dresser. If you have a landline phone in your bedroom, you'll want to disinfect that too along with any gaming systems.

Bedding and Headboard

Step One:

Although you probably clean your sheets quite frequently, now is a good time to deep clean the entire bed area. Start by stripping the bed until just the mattress is left. Most bedding can be washed so wash the bedding as you normally would. For a mattress cover or comforter, read the tag for any special instructions on how to wash it. Wash all the blankets, sheets, and pillowcases and then wash the pillows themselves. Look for any special instructions on the pillow itself but most can be washed on a cold, delicate cycle. Dry the pillows on a low heat setting or in a well ventilated area. Try to get the pillows completely dry to prevent mold or mildew from growing on them.

Step Two:

When cleaning an upholstered headboard, it's best to do so while the bed is stripped. Start by taking a vacuum hose and slowly go over the headboard. Doing this often will prevent dander and dust from getting stuck in the headboard. Next, sprinkle a generous amount of baking soda on a cloth and use patting motions to get the baking soda into the headboard. Leave the baking soda for a few hours and don't worry about the mess just yet. After a few hours, take the vacuum cleaner again and vacuum the headboard again. This easy trick will naturally clean and absorb any debris before being vacuumed up.

To clean a wooden headboard, prepare a solution of warm water, a few drops of dish soap, and a spoonful of baking soda. Use a microfiber cloth and gently rub this over the headboard to eliminate germs. The same mixture can be used to clean a metal headboard.

The Mattress

Step One:

Cleaning the mattress is super important as you spend about a third of your day in bed. Oils, dander, skin, and sweat can unfortunately seep into a mattress. The mattress should be cleaned at least once a month to preserve its freshness.

To start, vacuum the entire mattress using a hose. This is an important part so take your time. The vacuum will suck up a lot of debris and bring other dander to the surface to be cleaned in the next step.

Step Two:

In a bowl, mix a generous amount of baking soda and a few drops of an essential oil. Then, sprinkle the mixture over the entire mattress and let it sit for 45 minutes. After 45 minutes, vacuum the mattress again. Flipping your mattress once every three months is usually suggested.

Tip ☆

Investing in a mattress protector is definitely worth it and will make cleaning the mattress much easier and less frequent. Mattress protectors are usually plastic-like and will prevent debris from seeping into the mattress.

Floors, Rugs, and Trash

Step One:

Clean the bedroom floor by sweeping, vacuuming, and mopping (wooden floors). If you have a carpet cleaner, carve out some time to thoroughly clean them. Place all small rugs or master bathroom rugs into the washing machine on a cold, delicate cycle. Use low heat to dry. Always check the tags on the rugs for any special instructions. Larger rugs can be cleaned by using the same method as the mattress portion.

Step Two:

Empty any trash bins and clean them using a sponge and dish soap. Sprinkle baking soda at the bottom of the can to prevent odors.

Tip ☆

If you don't have a trash bin in your bedroom, consider purchasing one. Elegant and sleek designs are available. Having a trash bin nearby will keep your room cleaner than you think as trash can often pile up on lazy days.

Bedroom Checklist

Dust and Disinfect

1. Dust the corners and walls of the bedroom.
2. Dust on top of surfaces starting from the top and working your way down. Look for any furniture that has a horizontal top. Wipe down the sides as well as they can also collect dust.
3. Disinfect commonly touched items. This includes electronics, buttons, door handles, and knobs.

Bedding and Headboard

1. Remove all pillow cases, covers, blankets, comforters, etc. so that everything is gone but the mattress.
2. Wash all bedding, sheets, pillow cases, etc. as you normally would.
3. Wash the pillows themselves.
4. Wash the headboard using a method above.

The Mattress

1. After removing the sheets, vacuum the entire mattress using the hose.
2. Sprinkle baking soda over the mattress and let it sit for 45 minutes.
3. Vacuum the mattress again after 45 minutes.

Floors, Carpet, and Trash

1. Sweep, vacuum, and mop if you have hardwood floors. If you own a carpet cleaner or can hire a professional, have the carpets thoroughly cleaned.
2. Empty and clean trash bins.

Laundry Room

The laundry room is a vital area of a home. Laundry machines save a lot of time and effort. Although articles of clothing are the majority of what's being washed, other household items benefit from owning a washer. Towels, linens, bedding, fabrics, and pillows are some of the other items that frequent the laundry room. Having a clean space allows better productivity, but there's another reason to deep clean the laundry room. Because dirty items frequently come in and out, it's important to clean the laundry room space every so often.

The Washer

Step One:

To start, make sure everything is removed from the washing machine. Mix one part hot water with one part white, distilled vinegar. Use a rag to wipe down the entire exterior of the machine. Be sure to get all of the knobs for disinfection purposes. Next, focus on wiping down the inside. With the rag, wipe the cylindrical interior. If you can, pull back the rubber seal and clean the space inbetween. Remove any dispensers if possible and clean them and the areas around them as well. Scrub the agitator with a toothbrush or sponge. Be sure to get the lid as well.

Step Two:

Set the machine for the largest, longest, and hottest cycle. After the washer is full with water, which usually takes a minute or so, pour in four cups (950 mL) of bleach. Allow the washer to run for a minute or two and then pause the cycle. Let the water sit in the washer for one hour. After an hour, return to the washer and finish the cycle.

Step Three:

Now, follow the exact same process but this time pour in four cups (950 mL) of vinegar. This two-step process should be repeated about every three months to remove any debris or germs.

Tip ☆

Be sure to shake your clothes out to prevent any large particles from getting stuck in the washer. If necessary, rinse dirty items in the sink before placing them into the wash to prolong the life of the washer. Overtime, a buildup can occur and can prevent the washer from functioning properly. In addition, leave the lid open after a cycle so the machine can dry out. This will prevent most mildew or mold from growing.

Step Four:

Unplug the washing machine and vacuum the areas around the machine. Don't forget under the machine and the back wall of the machine, as dust tends to collect here.

The Dryer

Step One:

Locate the lint trap, and start by cleaning it out. Run your fingers along the screen or use a vacuum. Remove the trap if possible and clean using dish soap to remove any buildup. Dry the screen completely before returning it to the machine.

Step Two:

Take a cloth with a little dish soap and scrub the exterior and interior of the washing machine. This will remove any buildup or residue. A toothbrush can come in handy for hard to reach areas. Be careful not to use too much water and be sure to remove all the soap by gently rinsing with water. Dry the washer using a clean towel.

Tip ☆

Clean the lint filter after every use. Remove the filter about once a month and clean with soap and water to prevent buildup and prolong the life of the dryer.

Step Three:

Safely unplug the dryer. Move the dryer away from the wall and use a vacuum hose to eliminate any dust or lint. Pay attention to the wires and hose on the back of the dryer. Vacuum as much lint or debris on or surrounding the dryer as possible.

The Sink, Countertops, and Shelves

Step One:

If your laundry room or area has a sink, use dish soap and a sponge to thoroughly wash the sink. Follow the same procedure on the countertops using a cleaning solution of your choice. This is also a great time to disinfect any door handles, knobs, or bins. Wipe down and dust shelving units.

Windows and Floors

Step One:

Use a cleaner of your choice to clean the surface of the window. Don't forget the top ledge or bottom of the window where dust usually collects. Use a vacuum over any vents to eliminate dust.

Step Two:

Sweep, vacuum, or mop the floors to get rid of any dirt and germs. Like other sections mention, if you're able to get your carpet professionally cleaned, a deep cleaning is the time to do so.

Laundry Room Checklist

The Washing Machine

1. Wipe down the exterior and interior of the machine. Remove any dispensers and wash them as well. Don't forget to wipe the knobs of the machine for disinfection purposes.
2. Remove everything from the wash. Begin the first cycle with bleach, following the instructions above.
3. Run a vinegar cycle. Use the same directions from the bleach cycle. Afterwards, leave the lid open to allow the machine to dry out and prevent any mildew from growing.
4. Unplug the washer and use a vacuum hose to eliminate any debris on or around the washing machine. Pay attention to the back of the washer as dust tends to collect in this area.

The Dryer

1. Clean the lint trap by removing the debris and washing with dish soap.
2. Wipe the exterior and interior using a cloth, dish soap, or vinegar.
3. Unplug the dryer and use a vacuum hose to eliminate debris on or surrounding the dryer. Don't forget to vacuum under the dryer, or where it normally sits.

The Sink, Countertops, and Shelves

1. Wash and disinfect the sink.
2. Wash and disinfect the countertops.
3. Dust and disinfect any handles, knobs, or items commonly touched.
4. Dust all shelving and use a disinfectant if necessary.

Windows and Floors

1. Use a vacuum to go over any vents to eliminate dust.
2. Use a cleaner of your choice to clean the windows.
3. Sweep, vaccum, or mop the floors.

Children's Bedroom or Playroom

Living with small children or even teenagers can sometimes mean messes show up from no fault of your own. As children get older, implementing a helpful cleaning routine that they can understand can save you a lot of time. This section will go through some of the basics, and at the end of this section, you will see a kid friendly checklist. Many of the tasks described will be suitable for young children to accomplish. Older children can even use the cleaners suggested as they contain no harsh chemicals.

Dust and Disinfect

In a child's bedroom, things have a way of getting dirty quickly. Maybe the constant stir and commotion has something to do with it, but you'll want to keep your child's room as clean as possible to avoid illnesses.

To start, you'll want to dust everything. This could mean using a towel with dust spray or using a vacuum. A vacuum is great for cobwebs, hard to reach places, and vents. Be sure to dust pictures, ceiling fans, and light fixtures along with what you normally would dust in a bedroom.

Second, you'll want to disinfect everything and should do so quite regularly. Children are exposed to a lot of germs on a daily basis and don't always wash their hands. This means that germs have the ability to spread near and far. Disinfect everything from light switches to knobs to the door handle and other commonly touched items. Disinfect toys as much as possible so germs don't grow on them. Any stuffed animal toys should be put in the wash weekly. To clean plastic toys, the dishwasher, bathtub, or washing machine may be useful. Check the labels of the toys and don't expose electronics or toys with stickers to water. Those toys will need to be spot cleaned. Use a disinfectant wipe or vinegar to quickly sanitize toys.

Clean the Floors

After everything, and I mean everything, has been wiped down and cleaned, turn your attention to the floors. Sweep, vacuum, or mop the floors to add the finishing touch. This is a step you can easily teach your children as they get older.

Children's Room Checklist

My Job:

1. Make my bed.
2. Put my dirty clothes in the laundry basket.
3. Put my clean clothes in their respective drawers.
4. Pick up toys from my floor.
5. Put away my school supplies.
6. Put away toys.
7. Put books away.
8. Clean under the bed.

Parent's Job:

1. Hang up clothes in the closet.
2. Wash bedding and pillows.
3. Vacuum and flip mattress.
4. Wash stuffed animals.
5. Clean glass and mirrors.
6. Dust (cobwebs, vents, pictures, ceiling fan, light fixtures, curtain rods, shelves, windows, curtains, etc.)
7. Disinfect (door handles, dresser knobs, light switches, toys, etc.)
8. Vacuum or mop.

Entry Space and Doors

Although not everyone has a large entry space, it is likely that a similar space exists somewhere in your home. This area likely includes a space containing keys, shoes, coats, and doormats.

Doors

Step One:

Whether you have a dedicated entryway or not, every home or apartment has an entry door. Cleaning the front door is important as it gives the first impression of a home. Not only does the door collect particles from the inside, but also from the outside weather. Cleaning the entire door will prevent any particles from getting into your home. During allergy season, you might want to bump up how often you clean the doorways.

To clean an aluminum door, all that is needed is dish soap and warm water. Fill a bucket with warm water and add a few drops of dish soap. Then grab a sponge and get to work! Gently scrub the door and you'll be amazed what comes off. After all the debris is scrubbed, give the door a once over with water to get rid of any soap. Dry the door with a soft cloth to prevent any water marks. For a wooden door, the same method above can be used unless the wood is raw or unfinished. In this case, use a soft cloth to rub linseed oil over the door.

Step Two:

If your door has a glass or screen protector, you'll want to clean that next. Prepare the following solution in a glass spray bottle:

- ¼ cup (60 mL) white vinegar
- ¼ cup (60 mL) rubbing alcohol
- 1 tablespoon (9.4 grams) cornstarch

- 2 cups (500 mL) of water
- 10 drops essential oil (lemon, orange, lavender, etc.)

This is an excellent glass cleaner that can also be used on other parts of the home. Spray the mixture onto a microfiber cloth and wipe the glass surface. Avoid spraying directly onto the door as this is a glass cleaner. Use the spray to go over door handles as the cleaner also works as a disinfectant.

Step Three:

Take a vacuum hose and suck up any debris near the bottom of the door. You'll want to open the door completely to make for an easy work space. The vacuum hose is the most efficient tool for this part as there are many small spaces where dust/debris can get into.

After the debris is gone, use a sponge with a bit of dish soap to clean this part of the door. Use a towel to dry the area. This is an important area to clean, as much of the trapped particles can end up in your home.

Step Four:

Now, it's time to clean any doormats. There are two methods to clean them. Your outdoor mat is likely pretty sturdy and heavy duty. To clean this mat, shake it off in the grass and use a pressure hose to get rid of any stuck dirt. A few drops of dish soap may be necessary to get rid of grime but check the tag to see if there are any special instructions. Let the mat air dry in the sun.

Next, you likely have a rug or mat in the entryway inside of the home. Shake out loose debris first. Now, wash the rug/mat in the wash or with a sponge. Most mats can be washed using the cold, delicate cycle. Let the mat air dry in a well ventilated area or set in the dryer on the lowest heat setting.

Shoes and Coat Rack

Step One:

Start by taking an inventory of any shoes near the doorways. If your shoes are pretty clean, you can skip this step. When inspecting your shoes or the shoes of other family members, look to see if any are excessively dirty. You may not realize it but muddy shoes will dry and bits of dirt will end up in other areas of the house. Shake out such shoes outside before returning them to their dedicated space.

Step Two:

If you own a shoe rack, remove all of the shoes so it can be cleaned. Shoes have the ability to carry a lot of germs and debris that will likely end up on your shoe rack. Wiping it down every so often will prevent germs from spreading in your home. Use the disinfectant of your choice or a bit of white vinegar to eliminate germs. Return the shoes back to the rack after it is dry. You may wish to clean the bottom of your shoes as well during this step.

Step Three:

Take this time to use a disinfectant of your choice to wipe down the coat rack or coat hooks.

The Staircase

Step One:

If your staircase is carpeted, use a vacuum to suck up any dirt or dander. Use the vacuum hose to get into hard to reach areas. If you have a wood staircase, prepare the suggested solution found at the end of the book, or use a wood cleaner of your choice. Go over each step on the staircase and the railing to clean and shine the wood!

Step Two:

Spot clean any stains using equal parts of salt, borax, and vinegar. Start by using ¼ cup of each and then more as needed. Rub the paste over the stain and let it dry. Then use a vacuum to suck up the powder after it has dried.

Step Three:

After cleaning the stairs, it's now time to clean the railing or banister. Many traditional homes will have a wooden banister while newer, modern homes may have a different material. Either way, the staircase railing is bound to be infected by germs because of the traffic it receives. Constant touch and a fluctuation in temperatures will leave the railing feeling sticky and looking dull. The oils from constant touch can sink into the wood and leave behind residue, so it's important to deep clean the railing every so often.

For a wooden banister, start by using a microfiber cloth for a preliminary cleaning. Afterwards, take a sponge and a dab of Murphy Oil Soap. Equal parts of water and vinegar can also be used on finished or unfinished wood. If using the oil soap, use the rough side to gently exfoliate any grime off of the banister. If using the spray, spray the mixture onto the sponge and use the same method. This may take some time but luckily, cleaning the banister only needs to take place a few times a year. After a gentle scrub, use the soft side of the sponge to take away the dirt and soap.

For a stainless steel staircase railing, use warm water and a mild soap to gently scrub the railings. Dry afterwards with a microfiber towel.

Entry Space Checklist

Doors

1. Determine what type of material your front door is made of and clean using the method above.
2. Clean the glass and handles of the door.
3. Use a vacuum to suck up any debris in the bottom of the doorway. Use a sponge and a bit of dish soap to clean this part of the door. Use a soft towel to dry the area.
4. Shake out and wash outdoor and indoor rugs/mats using one of the methods above.

Shoes and Coat Rack

1. Shake out any dirty or muddy shoes outside.
2. Disinfect the shoe rack and the bottom of shoes if desired.
3. Wipe down the coat rack or hooks with disinfectant.

The Staircase

1. Take a vacuum to each staircase and use the vacuum hose to get into hard to reach corners.
2. Spot clean any stains on the carpet.
3. Clean the railings or banister using a method above.

PART 2: DECLUTTER AND ORGANIZATION

***

Now that your home has been thoroughly cleaned, it's time to turn your attention to any clutter. Clutter refers to the untidy collection of items. Having an abundance of clutter doesn't mean you have lots of junk or garbage. Although some of the items may fall into those categories, this section will help you figure out which items you no longer need. For this section, the main question you'll want to ask yourself is: What purpose does this item have? When sorting through the items in different rooms, you may find things you haven't seen in awhile. This is a great cue to show that these items are not serving a purpose and it's time to discard or donate them.

Getting rid of items is only the first step to a decluttered and organized home. The truth is, there will still be lots of items that are not needed even after a purge, and that's okay. This section will focus on how to create proper storage methods to keep your home organized and will show you how to create more valuable space. Many items can be stored in an easy-to-see, decorative way. In addition, if you don't wish to start any home renovation projects, this section will also give offer small suggestions that will help transform any space.

Each section will go through the most common rooms and areas of a home, and touch on the areas that likely need help. Each home is different, so you can customize the tasks how you wish, but this guide will give a basic framework for where to start. Many of the tips offered can be performed in an affordable, do-it-yourself manner.

Decluttering and organizing can take time. So do your best to get as much done in a short time period, but know that it's better to do these tasks sufficiently to help maintain the home in the future. After each room has been sorted through, you'll have the information and tips needed on how to maintain each space.

If you're ready to have an organized and clutter-free home then keep on reading!

CHAPTER 2 - Declutter and Organize by Room

Now that you have successfully deep cleaned your home, the next steps to a fantastic space is getting rid of clutter and creating a helpful organization system in each room. This chapter will take you through each room and give suggestions on items to throw away or donate. In addition, you will receive practical tips to help you organize and make the most of your space.

The Kitchen

The Pantry

<u>Step One:</u>

Earlier in the book, we discussed how to deep clean the pantry. During that time, you may have already started the organization process of your pantry. To organize the pantry, you'll want to make sure everything is grouped by category. Knowing where everything is will save a lot of time spent looking for items. Before doing this, or as you go, check each item to be sure it's not expired. Make a list of items to repurchase.

If you're organizing the pantry for the first time, start by grouping likewise items in a way that will be helpful to you. It is suggested that you group breakfast items near one another, and follow the same process for lunch and dinner items. Items used for every meal like spices and oils should be grouped in a separate space. You can also organize snacks by placing salt snacks in one bin and sweet snacks in another. Here is a list of categories to help you get started:

- Candy
- Cookies or dessert
- Sweet snacks
- Salty snacks
- Breakfast items (oats, syrup, peanut butter, etc.)
- Grains (rice, pasta, bread, etc.)
- Oils
- Soups or canned goods
- Baking
- Spices
- Lunch items
- Dinner items

Once all the items are in categories that make sense, consider installing some type of shelving or basket unit. You may already have containers or baskets that you can put to use. Budget dollar stores also carry containers that can be useful to you. The goal in organizing the pantry is to make your life easier and prevent further messes when in a rush. Place the items that are used the most in easy to reach areas. Items not commonly used should be placed higher up or further down in the pantry.

The next step is to label everything. Make the label large and visible enough so it's easy to see. This system will be helpful because instead of looking for one item in a sea of many, you'll be able to find it by simply going to the correct category.

Hang a clipboard or white board in the pantry. Write down items that are running low or items that are nearing their expiration date. You can also use this area to write your grocery lists.

Pots and Pans

Step Two:

Having organized cabinets will not only make a more enjoyable kitchen environment but will make cleaning up easier too. The first thing to think about is an area of your kitchen that needs some order. Are your pots and pans easy to access? Is your silverware sorted? Do you have to spend a lot of time looking through the cabinets to find containers or other items? Now that your kitchen has been deep cleaned, maintaining it will be so much easier with some organization.

Pots and pans can be an area that's hard to access. With so many pots and pans for different uses, storing them can be a challenge. Go through each pot and pan and look for any that are in need of serious replacement. Lots of wear and tear isn't healthy for a pot and severely scratched pans can be bad for your health in some cases. If you usually cook in large portions, donate some of the smaller pans that aren't used or store them in the pantry so they don't get in the way. If you cook in smaller portions, take the larger pans and store them elsewhere as well. Only a few pots and pans are truly needed to get rid of any overkill.

Pots and pans are best stored by creating a rack. A sturdy rack with hooks will also prevent them from rubbing up against each other, which will actually decrease the lifespan of the pot. Hanging pots is a nice design aspect that many can enjoy. If you don't prefer this type of design, the same can be achieved by hanging the pots and pans in the pantry or in a larger cabinet.

Containers and Measuring Cups

Step Three:

Now, it's time to sort through containers. Containers come in handy for storing food. Because there are so many options in regards to sizing and lids, this area of the kitchen can easily become disorganized. Start by sorting through tupperware and discarding old containers. Only keep what's absolutely needed to prevent clutter. To keep kids organized, use a dish rack and place all the lids, from smallest to largest, horizontally. Try to find a small or narrow dish rack so the containers can go beside it. Or, you can use small dividers to separate the lids from the containers. Always stack the same sized containers so they are easier to locate and aren't spread out.

For measuring cups, a similar method to pots and pans should be used. On the back of a cabinet door, insert small hooks. Then, label and hang the measuring cups from largest to smallest. Do this in a cabinet that is opened the least, but still in a convenient spot. To take it a step further, use a decorative pen or sharpie to write basic measurement conversions. These conversions will be helpful when you have dirty hands from baking so you don't have to pause and research.

Kitchenware

Kitchenware can cover a variety of items. It's time to look at the bigger picture to see where your kitchen could need some organizing. For some, storage and space is hard to come by. For others, too much space and storage creates unorganization. Whatever the case, get creative and try to organize items in a way that will be aesthetically pleasing and practical.

Plates, Cups, Silverware, and Cookware

Step One:

Depending on how much cabinet space you have, you may need to get creative and create space for your items. Not to worry, because creating space in a small kitchen can be done with style! Installing shelving is the simplest and easiest solution to combat limited storage. Exposed dishes and cookware is becoming trendy as well. If you do have cabinets, take this time to make sure plates are with plates, bowls are stacked, and everything is in its correct location.

Utensils and Tools

<u>Step Two:</u>

In kitchen drawers, install an organization container for silverware. These can be purchased for an affordable price and will help separate utensils. This is the time to get rid of or donate utensils that aren't getting any use. Spatulas and other tools are best stored on counter space. You can use a jar and place the tools vertically for easy access. Because kitchen tools have such different shapes, storing them in this way will save you time and effort trying to continuously organize them and will free up space.

Kitchen Knives

Step Three:

Kitchen knives can be stored a few ways, but should not be left in drawers to roam. The most common way to store knives is by using a butcher block. Another way to store knives is to purchase a bamboo knife block. If you prefer to store knives in a drawer, there are such blocks available for purchase. If you live with small children, this can be a great option. If you're dealing with limited counter space or drawers, and do not have small children, knives can be stored by installing a heavy duty magnetic strip. This can be done near the surface or even in a cabinet.

Refrigerator and Freezer

Step Four:

A great time to clean out the refrigerator and freezer is during a deep clean. Make sure no expired food is present first. If your refrigerator has a lot of storage space, you're in luck. If not, organizing and maintaining the refrigerator is still possible with a few easy steps.

If you have children, you'll want to create a special area for them. Doing so will help keep the refrigerator organized or at least keep any mayhem in one space. Creating a labeled snack drawer that kids can reach will be helpful because they won't have to move anything to find what they're looking for.

Second, invest in long, plastic containers that will fit different food items. Create labeled categories similar to those in the pantry. If your refrigerator already has a lot of storage, you can skip the plastic containers, although a few will come in handy. Some of the categories will include:

- Vegetables
- Fruit
- Protein/Meat
- Dairy
- Eggs
- Drinks
- Condiments
- Sauce

Having these items all in one place or in a container will make for easy removal and less time spent looking for items.

For the freezer, you'll want to follow a similar process. Make sure you only have what you need and eliminate clutter. Installing or purchasing removable bins will save you a lot of time organizing the freezer. Group similar items and put the items most used in easy access areas.

Kitchen Organization Checklist

The Pantry

1. Get rid of any garbage or expired items. Make a list of items that need to be repurchased.
2. Set each item into the proper category. Use the list above for reference.
3. Install a shelving or basket unit and use glass jars to organize the items by category.
4. Place the items most commonly used in easy to reach areas.
5. Label all baskets, jars, or shelves with the proper category.
6. Hang a clipboard or use a white board to write grocery lists.

Pots, Pans, and Containers

1. Go through each pot or pan and discard any damaged items.
2. Store less commonly used pots and pans elsewhere so they are not in the way.
3. Create a better mechanism for storing pots and pans by hanging them in a cabinet, on the kitchen wall, or in a pantry.
4. Go through and get rid of old containers. Keep only what you need.
5. Stack similar sized containers so they are easy to locate.
6. Use a dish rack or dividers to organize lids from smallest to largest.
7. Organize measuring cups on the back of a cabinet door. Use hooks and write basic measurement conversions.

Plates, Cups, Silverware, and Cookware

1. Organize dishes, plates, and bowls. Install additional shelving if necessary to create more space.
2. Install an organizer for kitchen utensils in a kitchen drawer. Donate or throw away any utensils that aren't getting used.

3. Store spatulas and other tools in a jar on top of the counter to free up space.

Kitchen Knives

1. Create a better mechanism to store kitchen knives by purchasing a butchers block or installing a magnetic strip as shown in the photograph above.

Refrigerator and Freezer

1. Get rid of any expired or unused items in the refrigerator and freezer.
2. Create a specific, easy to reach snack drawer for the kids.
3. Organize food into categories and use removable containers.
4. Follow the same process to organize the freezer.

Closets

If you're lucky, you'll notice you have quite a few closets around the house all serving a different purpose. This section will go over how to make the most of your closets and tell you how to create space in the places you wish you had a closet.

Bedroom Closet

Step One:

An organized, well maintained closet will make your life easier, especially for busy mornings. Whether you live alone or share a closet with someone else, you'll want to keep your items separate. For many, this means a his and hers closet. For those with limited space, the same effect can be achieved.

Start by going through your clothes. With each item, ask yourself how much use the item is getting. If you're holding on to any items that aren't getting worn regularly, now's the time to set them aside to donate later. Going through your clothes after every season or twice a year will help prevent clutter. Next, if you live in a climate where each season has a drastic temperature change, set those clothes aside for storage. If your closet is overflowing with space, store items of different seasons in the harder to reach areas until their time comes.

If you already have a ton of shelves, you can skip this step. However, if you find yourself opening your closet doors to just one or two racks, this step is for you. Although racks come in handy, not everything needs to go on a hanger. If you're able to install shelving, do so. You may need a bit of help for this part but the outcome will definitely be worth it. If you're not in the mood for a self-renovation project, there are other things that will prove helpful. In fact, there are many shelving options available for purchase that don't require any renovation. Baskets, linen cubes, and other bins are a great option. A shower caddie is an affordable way to organize accessories like sunglasses, hats, scarves, or even purses. You can also install hooks on the back of the closet door to hang ties, purses, or even jewelry.

If added shelving or bins is not possible due to the closet space, consider installing a fashionable clothes rod anywhere where space is available. Not only can this help with storage issues, but it can also add a trendy flair to your bedroom. Garment racks are also available for purchase and can showcase some of your favorite clothing items.

After adequate space is sorted, it's time to fold and hang any clothes to make the floor completely mess-free. Place any dirty clothes in the laundry to be washed. Place clothes that receive a lot of wear in an easy to access spot. You can organize your closet by color, occasion, or in order from thin to warm clothes. Generally, jeans, sweaters, comfortable clothes, or work clothes should remain near each other.

Children's Closet

Organizing a child's clothes can be quite challenging as children tend to grow so fast. Deciding what to keep and what to get rid of can be a tough. This section will help you organize and create a system for your children's clothes.

As a general rule of thumb, think about keeping eight outfits for summer and winter. Each outfit should include:

- Shirts (8 long-sleeve, 8 short-sleeve)
- Pants or shorts (8 each)
- Swimsuits (2)
- Jackets (winter, spring, fall, and summer)
- Shoes (formal, summer, sport, boots)
- Socks (7-14 pairs)

Remember that less clothing in rotation will yield less laundry during the week. When sorting through children's clothes, only keep what is helpful or needed. The above list is a guideline and it will differ depending on your climate and lifestyle.

For clothes that aren't in rotation or are too big, use labeled bins to categorize the clothes in storage. You can categorize and label by:

- Too big/outgrown
- Season
- By age
- Clothing article

If you receive hand-me-down clothing, it may be best to categorize the items by when they will fit or what size they are. By using smaller bins, you will limit the amount of clothing stored, which is helpful when avoiding clutter.

Store bins decoratively in linen baskets in the child's room or in storage bins elsewhere. Remember to make the label visible to save time finding items in the future.

Medicine Cabinet and Linens

Step Two:

Depending on where your additional closets are, they'll likely have similar functions. Medicine, cleaners, towels, and bedding are items found in many closets. This step will give helpful tips on how to organize these items.

For your medicine cabinet or area, start decluttering by throwing out old medicine. Most medicine will expire rather quickly so it's important to check the dates. Any medicine that you don't use, throw it away. If you have any exact replicas, combine the two. Remember to check the strength and only combine if they are the exact same. This will help save space. Next, use bins, baskets, racks, or an organizer to store medicine. You can sort medicine by the following categories:

- Pain relief
- Allergy
- Cough/cold
- Stomach
- Children's medicine
- First Aid
- Vitamins

Label the containers when storing the medicine or vitamins. Put more commonly used items towards the front of the closet or cabinet for easy access.

Move to the closet containing bedding. Odds are that the

bedding is folded, but could use a little tidying up. Discard any bedding that is not being used. Overtime, bedding needs to be replaced, so don't hold on to old sheets. Start by putting bedding into piles of the appropriate size. Twin, double, queen, and king-sized beds are the most common. If you have any pillow cases that belong with a set, add those to the correct pile. Any other pillow cases can be put in a separate pile. Duvet covers, blankets, or comforters can also have their own storage unit or be put into the correct size category. Use a basket or linen cubes to store the bedding. Remember to label the outside of the storage bin or basket.

Towels should be tackled next. Think about how many towels you truly need with how often you do laundry. Remember that larger towels, like those used after showering, are simply absorbing water and the towels generally stay clean as long as they dry well. Get rid of and donate excess towels including hand towels, face towels, and seasonal towels that aren't being used. Towels can be stored in a linen basket similar to bedding, or you can store them by rolling them. Rolling your towels will make for an easier grab and won't mess up the pile of other towels when taking from the bottom.

For other small miscellaneous items, store them in glass jars. Glass jars are helpful because they can store a lot without taking up a lot of space. Sponges, soap, q-tips, and cotton pads/balls are great items to store in a glass jar. A great thing about glass jars are that they are see-through, making finding items easier than ever, and also can add a decorative aspect to you bathroom when stored on the countertop.

Cleaning Closet

Step Three:

Although it's possible your cleaning products are in a cabinet, the same organizational tips can apply. Many of the cleaners suggested in this book require a glass spray bottle and many of the homemade cleaners are multipurpose. The cleaners mentioned in this book are natural, affordable, and are easily made. The truth is, just a few cleaners can get the job done, so throw away cleaners that aren't serving much purpose. You should only have a few cleaners, but make sure they are labeled for easy access. In addition, install hooks into the cleaning closet, cabinet, or in the laundry room. This will free up some space and will save you time when looking for specific tools.

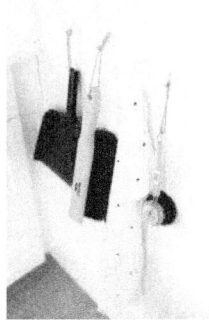

Closet Checklist

Bedroom Closet

1. Go through all items and donate anything not being worn regularly. Donate items that are the wrong size.
2. Set seasonal items aside for storage, or put them in an area away from your closet until their season comes.
3. If your closet could use some extra shelves, consider a do-it-yourself (DIY) project.
4. Use a shower caddie or hang small hooks for accessories and extra organization.
5. Consider installing a clothing rod or using a garment rack.
6. Place any dirty clothes in a laundry bin.
7. Hang and fold all clothes so the floor is clean.
8. Organize clothes by color, most worn, occasion, or by a category of your choice.

Children's Closet

1. Start by sorting through the clothes in the closet. Decide what to keep, discard, donate, or store.
2. Label stored clothes in a specific category.
3. Sort through clothes in drawers.

Medicine Cabinet and Linens

1. Sort through the area containing medicine. Discard any old medicine.
2. Seperate the medicine or vitamins into categories before placing them in their appropriate bin. Label the bins or basket.
3. Throw away old sheets and bedding.
4. Put all bedding into piles by size (twin, full, queen, king).
5. Put pillow cases with their matching sets, or form a new pile of pillow cases.

6. Place each folded pile into a large basket or linen cube. Label as needed.
7. Go through and discard old towels or towels not being used.
8. Roll towels and store them in a linen basket or cube.
9. Store smaller items in glass jars for easy access.
10. Hang items to save space.

Cleaning Closet

1. Throw away cleaners that are taking up space. Only a few cleaners are needed as many are multipurpose.
2. Hang items to save closet space and for easy access.

The Office

This section will be helpful for those who have a home office or work in an office environment. In addition, many have a space in their home to store important documents, do the bills, or have a space for children to do school work. These areas can often become disorganized or cluttered. Looking for papers or important documents can be challenging and consume a lot of time when things aren't in order. After you create a system using the following instructions, you'll be able to find everything quickly and will know how to maintain these areas for better use!

Sorting and Storing

Step One:

The first area to sort out should be the desk. Take everything on the surface of the desk and place it on the floor for sorting. Most of what you remove will be papers, notebooks, and pencils/pens. From the items on your desk, make separate piles of all documents, notebooks, or binders from the following categories:

- Medical
- Manuals
- Pets
- House
- Personal
- Auto
- Children

After sorting through the documents in the desk area, it's time to turn your focus to the drawers. Remove everything at once, or remove as you go through each item. Place the item into the appropriate category. Start thinking about where you have space to store these items. For important papers or items that are used frequently, use a file folder rack or holder. Label the outside of each rack in similar categories. Other papers should go into labeled binders. Label the binders in a way that's helpful for you, or by using a category above.

For other documents that you need but don't use often, store them in a space that will be out of your way. A filing cabinet will come in handy for this part. Purchase file folders and label them by categories, alphabetically, or in a way that's useful for you.

Binders, books, and notebooks can be stored on a shelf vertically or horizontally, depending on how much space you have. Whether this space is in an office or in another room, stored books can be an easy way to add design and dimension to a room. If you don't have shelves or don't wish to install them, you can also store items in a decorative box. Remember to shred and recycle anything you don't have room for or don't need.

The Desktop

Step Two:

Now that all documents and papers are sorted, it's time to turn to the desktop. Try to keep the desktop clean and clear. This will allow you to work more efficiently and not get distracted by clutter. Keep only useful items on the desktop. Pens, pencils, paper clips, and other small items can be stored in a decorative cup or glass jar. Glass jars add a sleek design element and they are see-through, therefore, making their content easy to locate. If you haven't already, invest in a planner or calendar and display it near the desk area. These items will promote organization and will serve as reminders for upcoming tasks.

Office Checklist

Sorting and Storing

1. Remove everything from the desk.
2. Place all items from on top of the desk into categories.
3. Remove everything from the drawers and sort them into the correct category.
4. Get rid of papers, books, and notebooks that aren't being used.
5. Documents or notebooks that are often needed should be stored in a file rack or in an easy to access area.
6. Place other documents in labeled binders or files and in a filing cabinet. Label as you deem necessary for easy access.
7. Store binders, books, or notebooks on a shelf or in a bin.

The Desktop

1. Choose what to store on the desk. Keep it minimal.
2. Use decorative cups and jars to store pencils, pens, paper clips, and other items.
3. Invest in a planner or calendar and keep it on your desk.

The Garage

Step One:

Over time, the garage is a place that suffers from clutter. A garage is not only used to house cars but usually other items as well. To clear out your garage, you'll want to sort through your items and decide what to keep. Here's a list of what you should go through:

- Chemicals
- Garden tools
- Sports equipment
- Kids toys
- Camping supplies
- Hand tools
- Electric tools
- Car fluids
- Paint supplies
- Holiday decor
- Winter gear
- Lawn chairs
- Beach equipment
- Hobby items
- Sentimental items
- Broken items
- Bikes and gear

For each category, start by locating all items. For instance, if you have holiday gear in the basement, garage, and attic, combine them and only store them in one place. It may take some time to locate everything but get started and do as much as you can. This project might spread over several rooms so it's okay to give yourself some time.

After you have located the items for each category, go through them. Discard anything that is broken, old, or unusable. Many of us tend to keep broken items or old furniture in the hopes of restoring them. If it's been some time and the item still isn't restored, take this opportunity to get rid of it so you can tackle other problems. Remember that for some categories, you only need one of each item. Don't hold onto 10 basketballs, 3 hammers, or 5 shovels unless they are serving a purpose. Only keep items that are truly useful to prevent clutter. Shelving, hooks, containers, and cabinets will serve useful depending on the items. The hooks shown below would be useful to hang any sport bags and seasonal sports gear.

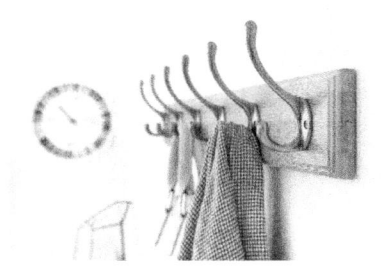

To store tools, installing a peg board or creating a wooden shelf, like the one shown below, may be useful. In the garage, anything that can be stored and also be seen is great because it will save time trying to find items.

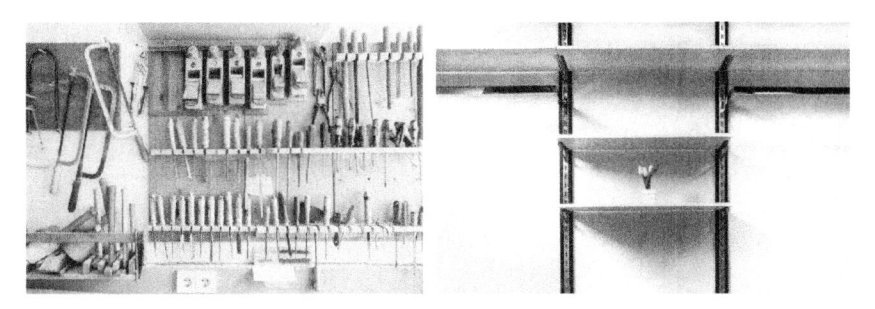

Garage Checklist

1. Start with one category at a time.
2. Locate all items and place them together.
3. Decide what you want to keep. Throw away or donate unused items. Discard broken items.
4. Discard items that you have more than one of unless they are serving a purpose.
5. Find an area to store the items.
6. Install hooks to hang items.
7. Place items in labeled bins.
8. Install shelving if necessary.

PART 3: LISTS

***

Below you will find helpful lists to help you clean, declutter, and organize your home. A variety of lists are given to help you accomplish tasks in a way that is suitable to your preference and lifestyle. It's suggested that you print these lists and check off tasks as they are completed.

CHAPTER 3 - Daily, Weekly, and Monthly Lists

Daily List

Kitchen

1. At the end of the day, make sure all dishes are placed in the dishwasher or are clean in the drying rack. Unload and put away dishes as needed.
2. Rinse the sides of the kitchen sink to prevent food from settling.
3. Wipe kitchen countertops after each meal or in the evening when kitchen use is finished. You can spot clean if only a small area is used.
4. Take out the garbage if it is full.

Living Room

1. Return all items to their correct spot. This includes books, dishes, clothing items, electronics, etc.
2. Fold blankets and fluff pillows.
3. Throw away any garbage.

Bathrooms

1. Wipe the bathroom sink to remove makeup stains, hairspray, toothpaste, or shavings.

2. Hang up towels.
3. Place dirty clothes in a laundry bin and clean clothes in the closet/drawer.

Bedroom

1. Take out any trash.
2. Make the bed.
3. Arrange and fluff pillows.
4. Put clothes in laundry bin or back into the closet or drawer.
5. Take any dishes to the kitchen.

Weekly Guide - 10 Minute Routines

Monday - **Kitchen**

1. Wipe kitchen appliances and stove
2. Wipe down the sink with disinfectant
3. Take out the trash as needed

Laundry: pillow cases and sheets

Tuesday - **Living Room**

1. Place trash into garbage
2. Remove any clutter
3. Dust shelves, fans, and furniture

Laundry: towels and rags

Wednesday - **Bathrooms**

1. Clean the mirrors
2. Wipe bathroom countertops and sink
3. Clean the toilet and surrounding areas

Laundry: lights and whites

Thursday - **Bedrooms**

1. Dust furniture, shelving, and electronics
2. Change the bedding
3. Pick up clothes and put them in the laundry or closet
4. Wipe mirrors

Laundry: darks

Friday - **Halls and Stairs**

1. Vacuum or mop the staircase
2. Remove all clutter and place items in their appropriate spaces

Saturday - **Floors**

1. Sweep all floors.
2. Vacuum all floors.
3. Mop all floors.

Sunday - **Disinfect**

1. Go around the house and disinfect door handles, appliances, and knobs.
2. Disinfect anything that is commonly touched like light switches, remotes, and game consoles.

Monthly Lists

The following lists will give you an idea of what tasks to do each month. It's suggested that you print the following lists and place them right next to your monthly calendar. These lists will help you keep your home clean and tidy all year long! If you don't have much time to set aside, these lists will be helpful in completely decluttering and deep cleaning in a year's time. The following lists are inspired by the The Typical Mom (2019), a blogger who specializes in organization.

January - **Purge**

Bedrooms

1. Go through clothes. Donate what doesn't fit or what's not worn often.
2. Throw away or donate old shoes.
3. Old hats and purses.
4. Old bedding.
5. Drawers and nightstand.

Bathrooms

1. Children's toys.
2. Empty bottles.
3. Old brushes and makeup.
4. Trash.
5. Expired perfumes.
6. Old towels.
7. Bath mats and rugs (clean or replace)
8. Medicine that is expired or not used.
9. Hair equipment and products.

Kitchen

1. Tupperware.
2. Cracked plates or glasses.
3. Mismatched sets.
4. Throw away expired or old food from the pantry, refrigerator, and freezer.
5. Go through cleaning supplies.
6. Replace pots and pans. Donate if in good condition.
7. Go through cookbooks.

Office

1. Shred old documents and receipts.
2. Go through keys.
3. Throw away old pens, pencils, or unused supplies.

Garage

1. Throw away broken items.
2. Throw away expired chemicals or dried paint.
3. Throw out unused holiday decor.
4. Go through boxes and bins.
5. Sort tools.

Children

1. Throw away broken toys.
2. Donate unused toys.
3. Donate outgrown beds or furniture.
4. Reconfigure and straighten room.

February - **Kitchen and Laundry Room**

The Refrigerator

1. Throw away expired food.
2. Combine similar condiments into one bottle. Throw away condiments you don't use.
3. Clean shelves.
4. Clean drawers.

The Freezer

1. Discard expired food.
2. Thaw and clean out entire freezer.
3. Replace filter if needed.
4. Discard damaged ice trays or containers.

Kitchen

1. Go through oven mitts. Replace and discard as needed.
2. Go through tablecloths. Replace and discard as needed.
3. Go through dishes. Get rid of chipped or miscellaneous dishes. Donate those in good condition.
4. Discard old holiday serving dishes that you don't use.

Laundry Room

1. Go through chemicals and detergents. Throw out items you don't use or that are expired.
2. Clean the inside of the washer.
3. Clean the inside of the dryer.
4. Clean the lint trap.
5. Clean lint from dryer hose.

March - **The Garage**

Declutter

1. Dried Paint
2. Expired chemicals
3. Broken tools
4. Damaged or unused sports equipment
5. Broken or unused bikes
6. Broken or old camping gear
7. Broken or unused coolers
8. Holiday decor
9. Children's toys
10. Backpacks or sports gear

Clean

1. Dust shelves
2. Clean the floor and any spills
3. Inside of buckets
4. Vacuum floor and smaller spaces
5. Garage refrigerator or freezer

Organize

1. Holiday decor
2. Chemicals
3. Tools
4. Garden Tools
5. Cleaning supplies

April - **Spring Cleaning**

Bathroom Cleaning

1. Bathtub jets
2. Interior of bathtub
3. Deep clean the shower including the showerhead and drains
4. Bathroom floors
5. Baseboards
6. Interior and exterior of toilet
7. Sinks
8. Interior and exterior of cabinets
9. Mirrors
10. Shower curtain and liner
11. Window
12. Window curtains
13. Bath mats or rugs
14. Sort through the medicine cabinet

Bedroom Organizing

1. Go through clothing and shoes. Donate or discard old/unworn items.
2. Go through drawers and nightstands.

Bedroom Cleaning

1. Pillows
2. Mattress (flip the mattress)
3. Carpet or rugs
4. Windows and their curtains
5. Walls and baseboards

May - **The Office**

Office Cleaning

1. Walls and baseboards
2. Desk
3. Inside drawers
4. Books and shelves
5. Computer area
6. Printer
7. Window and curtains
8. Carpet and rugs
9. Chairs
10. File cabinet

Declutter

1. Shred unneeded documents
2. Broken electronics
3. Pens and pencils
4. Old bills
5. Filing cabinet

June through September - **Summer Cleaning**

Kitchen

1. Cupboards (interior and exterior)
2. Refrigerator contents
3. Freezer contents
4. Change lining in drawers or wash drawer organizers
5. Inside the pantry and junk drawer

Bedrooms

1. Blanket
2. Pillows
3. Clutter in drawers
4. Under the bed
5. Closets
6. Desk
7. Ceiling fans

Bathrooms

1. Toilet (interior and exterior)
2. Bathtub and shower
3. Under the sink areas
4. Throw away unused or old items
5. Shower head and faucet
6. Drains

Garage

1. Garden equipment
2. Tools
3. Shelves
4. Lawnmower basket
5. Floor

October - **Fall Cleaning**

Linens

1. Go through old sheets.
2. Throw away stained towels.

3. Get rid of unused towels and bedding.
4. Go through medicine and discard expired items.
5. Go through makeup.
6. Discard old blankets.

Closets

1. Throw away old or unused jackets.
2. Go through umbrellas.
3. Get rid of broken hangers.
4. Go through shoes. Store summer shoes, throw them away, or donate.
5. Go through purses.
6. Get rid of clutter and garbage.

Laundry Room

1. Clean inside of washing machine.
2. Clean interior of dryer.
3. Clean out the dryer hose.
4. Clean floors.
5. Clean drains.
6. Clean laundry room sink.
7. Get rid of expired or unused items.
8. Clean shelves.
9. Get rid of broken laundry bins.

November - **Basement and Office**

Basement

1. Go through holiday decor.
2. Go through regular decor.

3. Get rid of any trash or clutter.
4. Go through books. Donate what you don't need.
5. Get rid of broken items.
6. Throw away expired chemicals or old paint.
7. Prepare and go through winter gear.
8. Replace damaged wires.

Office

1. Shred old bills.
2. Organize tax documents.
3. Go through office supplies and tools. Keep only what you use.
4. Get rid of unused electronics or broken electronics.
5. Go through desk drawers.
6. Clean computer monitors and area surrounding.
7. Dust furniture.
8. Go through cords.

December - **Kids Items and Garage**

Kid's Items

1. Go through broken toys.
2. Donate unused toys.
3. Go through dress-up clothing.
4. Go through regular clothing and donate items that don't fit.
5. Organize toys into shelving or container system.
6. Go through puzzles and games.
7. Go through movies and books.

Garage

1. Donate used sports equipment.
2. Go through winter gear and summer gear.
3. Organize tools.
4. Clean out unused tools.

☆ *If you have gotten this far and have achieved more than you thought possible, please consider leaving a short review for the book on Amazon, it means a lot to me! Thank you.*

CHAPTER 4 - Seasonal and Deep Cleaning Lists

If you prefer to clean your house throughout the year, this chapter is for you! The first list will guide you through a seasonal clean. This list can be used for spring, summer, fall, and winter cleaning; or, this list can be used every four months throughout the year. The second list will guide you through a deep clean for whenever it's needed in your home.

All Seasons List

Kitchen

1. Deep clean the oven.
2. Clean the microwave.
3. Deep clean the refrigerator.
4. Deep clean the freezer.
5. Deep clean the coffee machine.
6. Condition or seal countertops.

Bedrooms

1. Wash pillow cases.
2. Wash comforters, duvets, and blankets.
3. Vacuum the mattress.
4. Flip the mattress.

Living Room and Bathroom

1. Wash pillows.
2. Deep clean the shower/bath.
3. Deep clean shower curtains/plastic liner. Replace if necessary.
4. Deep clean toilet bowls and sinks.

Laundry Room

1. Vacuum around washer and dryer. Move the machines to get underneath.
2. Deep clean the washer.
3. Deep clean the dryer.

All Rooms

1. Clean the carpet.
2. Clean rugs.
3. Clean curtains.
4. Vacuum underneath furniture.
5. Clean fireplace.
6. Clean upholstery and furniture.
7. Dust blinds.
8. Clean windows.
9. Scour sinks.
10. Dust walls.

The Ultimate Deep Cleaning

Kitchen

1. Clean the inside of appliances (oven, microwave, toaster, refrigerator, freezer, etc.).
2. Organize cabinets and pantry. Throw out expired items.
3. Go through the refrigerator. Throw out expired items or ones not used.
4. Dust light fixtures.
5. Wipe down countertops.
6. Wipe backsplash.
7. Wipe the outside of appliances and cabinet doors.
8. Clean and scour the sink.
9. Clean fixtures, doorknobs, and handles.
10. Wipe down walls.
11. Seal or condition countertops.
12. Sweep, mop, or vacuum floors.

Bathrooms

1. Clean interior of toilet.
2. Clean exterior of toilet.
3. Wipe down lid, top, and handle of toilet.
4. Wipe down counter space.
5. Wipe down sinks.
6. Wipe down fixtures in sink and shower.
7. Organize items in cabinet. Throw away what you don't need and what's expired.
8. Scrub bathtub/shower.
9. Organize medicine.
10. Clean mirror.

11. Clean windows and blinds.
12. Wipe down walls and baseboards.
13. Disinfect door handles and knobs.
14. Sweep, mop, or vacuum floors.

Living Areas

1. Dust all furniture and shelving.
2. Clean furniture, decorative pillows, and curtains.
3. Clean carpets and rugs.
4. Sort magazines and books. Throw away what you don't need.
5. Dust light fixtures and fans.
6. Polish furniture.
7. Clean windows and blinds.
8. Dust decorative items.
9. Vacuum vents.
10. Condition hardwood floors (optional).
11. Sweep, mop, or vacuum floors.

Dining Room

1. Wash table cloths.
2. Dust light fixtures.
3. Dust furniture and any shelving.
4. Wipe down walls and baseboards.
5. Dust decor.
6. Clean windows, blinds, and curtains.
7. Sweep, mop, and vacuum floors.

Bedrooms

1. Dust and polish furniture.

2. Dust decor.
3. Dust fans and fixtures.
4. Go through closets and organize. Get rid of unwanted items.
5. Dust and mop under the bed.
6. Disinfect light switches, knobs, and door handles.
7. Wash curtains.
8. Clean the mattress.
9. Flip the mattress.
10. Replace old bedding.
11. Wipe walls and baseboards.
12. Clean windows and blinds.
13. Sweep, vacuum, or mop floors.

Office

1. Dust furniture.
2. Wax or polish furniture (optional).
3. Dust keyboard, mouse, computer, and monitor.
4. Disinfect keyboard, mouse, computer, and monitor.
5. Wipe down the desk.
6. Wipe down the drawers.
7. Clean out files and the filing cabinet.
8. Sort through documents and throw away what you don't need.
9. Organize paperwork and bills.
10. Shred documents.
11. Wipe down windows and blinds.
12. Clean curtains.
13. Disinfect desk chair.
14. Disinfect door handles and knobs.

15. Sweep, mop, or vacuum floors.

Garage

1. Organize chemicals, sports equipment, tools, seasonal items, bikes, camping gear, etc.
2. Get rid of unused items.
3. Install shelving, hooks, or storage system.
4. Dust shelves.
5. Vacuum the floors and hard to reach areas.
6. Disinfect commonly touched areas.
7. Power wash the floors.

Miscellaneous

1. Clean and organize the entryway.
2. Clean entryway floors.
3. Deep clean front door and other doors. Clean the areas surrounding.
4. Organize coat closet.
5. Clean all pet items (toys, bowls, leashes, litter box, etc.)
6. Vacuum all vents.

CHAPTER 5 - All about Cleaners

When cleaning a home, we expect certain promises from a cleaning product. A cleaning product should remove germs, stains, dirt, and leave the area better than it was before. While many cleaners fulfill their promises, what you don't realize is the effect it's taking on your health and environment.

Natural cleaning products have become popular over the years, and for good reason. Harsh cleaners like bleach, ammonia, and others should be used with caution. A study found that using bleach just once a week increases the risk of chronic obstructive pulmonary disease (COPD) by a third (Person, 2017). If you live alone, you're exposing yourself to harsh chemicals that are known to be harmful to your health. Likewise, children and significant others are exposed as well if you live in a family environment. According to Healthline, "Bleach, ammonia or quaternary ammonium compounds (a type of disinfectant), phthalates, and many volatile organic compounds (VOCs) in typical cleaning products have all been linked to respiratory illnesses, including asthma, according to Allen Rathey, principal of The Healthy Facilities Institute" (Fischer, 2017). Cleaners have been a popular research topic within the last decade due to new findings. Household cleaners that contain unnatural chemicals have been proven to cause cancer in animal mammary glands and other studies have found a possible link between those chemicals and breast cancer in women (Relaxnews, 2011). Whether or not you suffer the immediate or long term effects, know that a similar result can be achieved with natural products; products you likely already have!

Household cleaners aren't commonly thought of as pollutants, but the truth is many have a negative impact on the environment. The chemicals found in common household cleaners have been classified as a volatile organic compound. Ammonia, nitrogen, and phosphorus are the compounds most commonly found in household products. These compounds are found in dishwasher detergent, glass cleaner, and sanitizing/degreasing agents. Because these products are being washed down the drain one way or another, the compounds frequently enter the water systems. After the cleaner travels down the drain, the water travels to the sewage system and later enters rivers, lakes, and large bodies of water. Although water is usually treated and cleaned through a water plant, many of these chemicals can't be thoroughly removed because of their volatile nature. Contaminated runoff affects plants, natural bacteria, and animals. Furthermore, household cleaners can and do pollute the air. After being trapped in your home, chemicals escape into the atmosphere when windows or doors are opened. This creates air quality issues and smog problems. Many states have taken the step to reduce the quantity of VOCs allowed in products for smog problems specifically.

To avoid environmental problems, it's recommended that you make the switch to natural cleaners. Not only is it better for you and your family, but also for the environment and animals. The same pristine effect can be achieved with the natural products suggested in this guide.

What You Should Know

You may have noticed that vinegar and baking soda are commonly mentioned throughout this guide. In fact, they are suggested so often you may be wondering what's so special about them?

Vinegar is a natural cleanser that is also powerful for cleaning grease, grime, and mineral deposits. Vinegar's acidity is able to kill germs, making vinegar the perfect disinfectant. Vinegar can kill germs like salmonella, E. coli, and gram-negative bacteria. Gram-negative bacteria is responsible for making you sick. Because vinegar kills 100% of gram-negative bacteria, vinegar is a natural, sufficient cleaner for disinfecting. In the lists portion of this chapter, you'll find a printable list detailing what vinegar should be used for and what to avoid when cleaning with vinegar.

Baking soda is a versatile product. Baking soda is safe for consumption while also being able to fight rust and tarnish, making it a pretty unique substance. Baking soda has been used for ages. What many don't know is that baking soda is actually salt. Baking soda is the opposite of acidic and falls on the basic side of the pH scale. Baking soda is an absorbent and works like an air freshener, except it doesn't contain chemicals and toxins like your basic aerosol. Baking soda contains fine particles that are perfect for a gentle exfoliation.

Baking soda and vinegar is a common cleaner mentioned frequently throughout the sections of this guide. Baking soda and vinegar combined make the perfect cleaner for eliminating grease, odors, stains, and bacteria. The two substances react with each other to create a gassy, carbon dioxide solution. Again, the power of these two together will have you saying goodbye to harmful, toxic cleaners. Even better, the two ingredients can be used on many surfaces in your home and cost a fraction of the price in comparison to store bought cleaners.

Another item frequently mentioned is essential oils. Essential oils are compounds extracted from plants. The oil contains a high concentration of the properties of which they are found in. Oils are used for their aromatherapy properties but also may have some health benefits. Essential oils are a great way to still enjoy fragrances in a natural, nontoxic way. Because essential oils are derived from plants, many of their microbial benefits are carried over. This means that essential oils can have the same benefits as their source. Lemon, for example, is known for its antiviral and antibacterial properties. Lemon, as an essential oil, also has the same properties and is potent enough to act in the same way which can prove useful for cleaning. Only high quality oils should be used as some contain synthetic chemicals, fragrances, or oils. In the list section, you will find common essential oils and their claims.

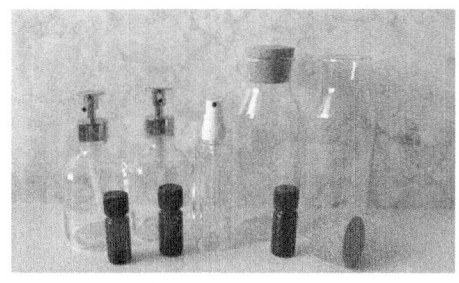

Natural Cleaners - Printable Lists

Vinegar

Vinegar Don't List

Vinegar is acidic and these surfaces should not be cleaned with vinegar. For most, a small amount of dish soap will do the trick. See the cleansers list for more information on what to use on these surfaces.

- Granite
- Marble
- Soapstone
- Kitchen knives
- Clothes iron

With Caution:

Use a small amount or be sure the vinegar is diluted. Porous surfaces can be damaged by undiluted vinegar.

- Hardwood floors
- Stone floors
- Grout

Safe with Vinegar:

These are the surfaces you should definitely use vinegar on. These surfaces respond well to vinegar and will make cleaning easy!

- Dishwasher
- Washing machine
- Refrigerator
- Carpet
- Toilet bowl

- Clogged drains
- Humidifier
- Sticky items
- Windows
- Mirrors
- Shower head and faucets
- Hard water stains
- Soap scum
- Garbage disposal
- Microwave
- Stainless steel
- Fabrics
- Cutting boards

Baking Soda

Baking soda is a great exfoliant that can absorb odors and get rid of stains. Baking soda can be used alone or mixed with a little water to create a paste when scrubbing. Because baking soda is an exfoliate, you'll want to use caution or avoid using on delicate surfaces.

Uses for Baking Soda:

- Air freshener
- Whiten and clean laundry
- Oven
- Stained coffee cups
- Stained marble
- Grease stains
- Kitchen tiles

- Clogged drains
- Tarnished silver
- Microwaves
- Bathroom tiles
- Toilets
- Showers
- Bathtubs
- Bathroom sinks
- Burnt stains on pots/pans
- Laundry booster
- Garbage disposal
- Mattress
- Coffee pot

Baking Soda is Not Safe For:

- Gold-plated serving pieces
- Marble
- Glass
- Ceramic stove top
- Wood furniture

Baking Soda and Vinegar Uses

The most common ratio to use, as a rule of thumb, is one part baking soda to two parts vinegar. Reference vinegar and baking soda sections to see what surfaces you should not use this combination on.

Baking Soda and Vinegar Uses:

- Carpet stains

- Polish silverware
- Stainless steel sink
- Unclog drains
- Tile floors
- Concrete
- Grout
- Toilet bowl
- Shower head
- Laundry

Essential Oils

Whether you're incorporating essential oils into your cleaners for their added benefits, or just adding a natural scent, essential oils are extremely useful and versatile. When cleaning with essential oils, never put them into plastic. Always use a glass bottle as essential oils can extract impurities, especially when placed in plastic. The following list will tell you the most common cleaning essential oils and their purpose according to Allison Hess (2018), a blogger for the popular website Home Revolution.

Types of Essential Oils and Claims:

- **Lemon**
  - Antiviral and antibacterial
  - Helps cut grease
  - Helps remove sticky, greasy substances

- **Tea Tree**
  - Also known as Melaluca
  - Antimicrobial, antibacterial, antifungal, and antiviral
  - Great for an all-purpose cleaning spray and mildew

- *Lavender*
  - Antibacterial and fights odors
  - Great for adding a pleasant aroma
  - Multipurpose

- *Eucalyptus*
  - Antiseptic, anti-inflammatory, and antimicrobial
  - Great for fighting allergy symptoms
  - Fights mold and mildew

- *Wild Orange*
  - Filled with vitamin C
  - Enzymes eat and prevent bacteria
  - Fights grease
  - Great alternative to lemon in regards to the aroma

- *Peppermint*
  - Antibacterial and antifungal
  - Rodent and pest repeller
  - Good for glass or mirrors because it gives streak-free shine
  - Invigorating and energizing aroma

- *Cinnamon*
  - Considered the spice of protection and prosperity
  - Kills serious viruses and bacteria
  - Antibacterial and antiseptic
  - Fights mildew, mold, and fungi
  - Inviting aroma

- ***Pine***
  - Kills germs and bacteria
  - Great alternative to lemon
  - Fresh and clean aroma

DIY Cleaners By Surface

Wood

- *1 cup water (237 mL)*
- *½ cup vinegar (118 mL)*
- *2 tablespoons of olive oil (30 mL)*
- *10 drops essential oil (lemon)*
- *5 drops essential oil (cedarwood)*

Laminate

- *1 cup water (237 mL)*
- *½ cup white vinegar (118 mL)*
- *2 teaspoons of olive oil*
- *10-15 drops essential oil (orange, lemon, etc.)*

Oven

- *½ cup (90 grams) baking soda*
- *A few drops of water*

Garbage Disposal

- *1 cup (180 grams) baking soda*
- *1 cup (237 mL) white vinegar*

Silverware Polish

- *1 tablespoon (14.5 grams) baking soda*
- *1 tablespoon (17 grams) sea salt*
- *½ cup (118 mL) white vinegar*

Upholstery Stains

- *½ cup (118 mL) dish soap*
- *1 cup (237 mL) hydrogen peroxide*

Leather

- *½ cup (118 mL) white vinegar*
- *¼ cup (54 grams) coconut oil*
- *½ teaspoon (7 mL) dish soap*
- *10 drops* essential oil (orange, lemon, etc.)

Furniture or Fabric

- *½ cup (118 mL) rubbing alcohol*
- *½ cup (118 mL) vinegar*
- *5 drops essential oil (orange, lemon, etc.)*

Disinfectant Wipes

- *2 cups (500 mL) warm water*
- *1 cup (237 mL) rubbing alcohol*
- *A few drops of essential oils*
- *A few drops of dish soap*
- *One paper towel roll*
- *Glass container that fits the rolls*

Toilet Cleaner

- *½ cup (90 grams) baking soda*
- *½ teaspoon (3 grams) tea tree oil*
- *1 cup (237 mL) white vinegar*
- *A few drops of essential oil*

Glass and Mirrors

- *½ cup (118 mL) white vinegar*
- *¼ cup (60 mL) rubbing alcohol*
- *1 tablespoon (9.4 grams) cornstarch*
- *2 cups (500 mL) water*

- *10 drops essential oil (lemon, orange, etc.)*

CHAPTER 6 - Moving Guide and Checklist

Moving can be time consuming and take a lot of work. Although the process is not always enjoyable, the outcome is usually worth it! Whether you're moving into your first home or apartment, or move regularly, this section will give helpful advice and checklists to aid in the process. The first part of the section will give practical tips on what to pack while the second section will put all of the instructions in an easy to read, printable list.

Moving Instructions

Step One:

Before moving, you should always set a date. This may seem like an obvious step, but having a concrete date will help you create a better schedule. A few weeks before moving, you'll want to enlist some help or schedule moving trucks/vans. Ask able friends and family if they're willing to help and reward them with drinks or dinner. Moving can be a fun process and can be a great way to catch up with friends and family.

There are a few additional steps to take before moving as well.

Notify:

- friends
- family
- employer
- physician
- school
- banks
- insurance company

Forward:

- cable
- utilities
- mail
- Internet or wifi

Step Two:

The first thing that should be done in preparation for a move, is to survey your belongings. Because each item has to be packed in a box, you have the perfect opportunity to get rid of unneeded items.

The declutter section of this guide will be a helpful resource. However, below is a general overview of items that should be sorted through. You can declutter these items as you go, or by room.

- *clothes*
- *shoes*
- *seasonal clothing items (jackets, hats, scarves, gloves, swimsuits, etc.)*
- *books, dvds, cd's*
- *games*
- *toys*
- *decor*
- *seasonal decor*
- *furniture*
- *pictures and memorabilia*
- *bedding*
- kitchenware

Many of these items can be donated or sold if in good condition. Moving can be an exciting time, especially when upgrading. Don't be afraid to let old items go to make room for newer items.

Step Three:

Now that everything's been sorted through and you have the items you want in your new home, it's time to start packing. Cardboard boxes are commonly used for this part and can be the most affordable. Many grocery stores or rummage sites will have these for free. Try to get as many boxes as possible weeks before moving so you can chip items away, little by little.

The best way to pack items is by room. At the end of this chapter, you will find a detailed list for each room, regarding what to pack. You'll obviously want to take all of your items, but having a list with instructions can speed up the process and make your time spent more efficient.

To make boxes easy to access, you can color code them and label them. Color coding them doesn't have to be difficult or take up a lot of your time. Color coding can help with an array of situations. For example, you may want to put a red piece of tape on breakable items. Placing a piece of red tape on the top of boxes will let everyone know to be careful with the box, and not to drop it. You can also mark important items that should be unloaded first using color coding. Even if the items don't belong in the same room, the color will tell you that it needs to be unpacked first.

Whether you choose to implement color coding or not, you should always label boxes by room and their items. The labels can be specific or general, but in a way that's useful for you.

Make a seperate box for items you will need right away. A few cups, toothbrushes, and towels are items that will come in handy right away. Also keep important documents and information in a safe, accessible place.

Step Four:

When you arrive at the new location, you'll want to bring all the boxes into the house as soon as possible. To help move in more efficiently, you should take each box to it's appropriate room right away. This will help keep you organized and will prevent the overwhelming feeling of tons of boxes. Staying organized is the key to a successful and efficient move.

Unpack the essential items in each room first. This part will be even easier if the essential boxes are color coded. Decor and items used less frequently should be unpacked last. Don't feel like you have to get everything done right away. It's best not to procrastinate, but give yourself some time to unpack properly. Use the organization portion of this book for advice on how to create a well functioning space.

Kitchen items, bedding, and toiletries should be set up right away to help you function through the packing process. A list at the end of this section will show you what to leave out for the first few days. These items will be necessary for living. Music or your favorite TV show in the background can make unpacking an enjoyable experience.

Moving Checklist by Room

Before the Move:

1. Enlist or hire help if needed.
2. Forward and notify using the list above.
3. Sort through the items of your home using the list above before throwing them into a box. Donate, sell, or discard unused or damaged items.
4. Pack items into their respective boxes. Reference the checklists below for each room.
5. Label and use a color coding method on boxes if desired.
6. Set aside important documents and personal items you'll need right away.

During the Move:

1. Call and make sure your new home has utilities set up.
2. Organize boxes in the moving van by room, or items you'll need first.
3. When removing the boxes, take them to their appropriate room right away.

Unpacking and Organizing:

1. Unpack the items that are needed first/the essentials. This step should be easy if color coded.
2. Take your time, but don't procrastinate unpacking. Use the organization tips in this guide to create a well functioning space.

What to Pack

Kitchen

1. Cups/mugs
2. Napkins
3. Silverware
4. Knives
5. Towels
6. Appliances (optional)
7. Kitchenware
8. Trash can/bags
9. Cleaners
10. Tupperware
11. Table
12. Chairs
13. Decor
14. Pantry items
15. Refrigerator items
16. Freezer items
17. Alcohol

Bedroom

1. Bedding
2. Mattress
3. Bed (headboard)
4. Side tables/night stand
5. Furniture
6. Blankets, pillows, comforters
7. Picture frames

8. Decor
9. Anything under the bed
10. Laundry basket
11. Mirror
12. Storage bins

Closet

1. Undergarments and socks
2. Pants
3. Dresses
4. Ties
5. Shorts and skirts
6. Sweaters and sweatshirts
7. Seasonal wear
8. Pajamas
9. Shoes
10. Jackets
11. Formal wear
12. Jewelry
13. Glasses
14. Accessories

Office

1. Decor
2. Pencils, pens, markers
3. Notebooks and binders
4. Important papers
5. Furniture
6. Desk
7. Folders

8. Planners
9. Office supplies
10. Computer and electronics
11. Filing cabinet

Electronics

1. Chargers
2. Printer
3. Power strips
4. Extension cords
5. Hard Drive
6. Computer
7. Phone
8. Tablets and Ipad
9. Game systems
10. TV
11. Alarm clock

Bathroom

1. Shower items
2. Hair products and tools
3. Iron
4. Toothbrush and toothpaste
5. Towels
6. Razor
7. Makeup
8. Soaps
9. Lotions
10. Detergent and laundry items
11. Medicine cabinet

Living Room

1. Furniture
2. Electronics
3. Decor
4. Rugs and carpets
5. Sofas
6. Lamp fixtures
7. Memorabilia

Garage

1. Chemicals
2. Tools
3. Gardening items
4. Car care items
5. Seasonal outdoor decor
6. Holiday decor
7. Beach equipment
8. Lawn chairs
9. Sports equipment
10. Bikes and bike gear
11. Camping gear
12. Winter sports gear
13. Shoes
14. Paint

Moving Items to Keep Handy

For Unpacking

1. Scissors
2. Box cutter
3. Sharpie
4. Basic cleaning supplies
5. Garbage bags
6. Screwdriver
7. Wrench
8. Drill

Toiletries

1. Toilet paper
2. Hand soap
3. Towel
4. First Aid

Eating

1. Paper plates
2. Napkins
3. Water bottles and glasses
4. Silverware
5. Snacks
6. Food for pets

Sleeping

1. Bedding
2. Pajamas
3. Toiletries

4. Change of clothes

Electronics

1. Laptop
2. Cell phone
3. Chargers

Kids

1. Bedding
2. Pajamas
3. Favorite stuffed animal and blanket
4. Night light
5. Toothbrush and toothpaste
6. Change of clothes
7. Entertainment (toys or games)

Paperwork

1. Important phone numbers
2. Bills
3. Passport
4. Private information

CHAPTER 7 - Decluttering Technology

Believe it or not, technology serves a huge role in most of our lives. Cell phones and computers are likely used on a daily basis depending on your job or lifestyle. Just how a room frequently used gets dirty or disorganized, so can our devices. This section is all about decluttering your phone and computer. Technology can also be a great resource to help you stay organized and keep you on track. We'll show you the top 10 apps that will help you manage and organize your daily life better!

How to Declutter Your Computer and Phone

Below are the five steps you should take to clean up your computer. Cleaning out your computer every so often will keep systems fresh and running as fast as possible. Although each computer is different, below are the five different areas you should be looking at to organize your computer or laptop.

Computer or Laptop

Step One:

The first step to organizing your computer is to sort through the various programs downloaded. Installed programs can be using up storage space and slowing your computer down. If you only use the program once or twice a year, it's best to download it as you need it, instead of storing it on your computer.

Step Two:

The next step is to go through your files. It's likely you have stored documents that are no longer needed and old. Getting rid of these will free up space and you'll be able to find what you're looking for much quicker. You can also store files on a seperate flash drive to save space.

Step Three:

To organize your files, create different folders to place them in. You should categorize them in a way that makes the most sense to you. Some examples would be work, finance, home, kids, pictures, important documents, etc. Your desktop will look much cleaner and you'll know exactly where to find specific files.

Step Four:

You should regularly empty your recycle bin. If not, take this time to do so. You may not realize it, but the items in your trash can still take up a lot of space on your computer and won't get fully deleted until the trash is emptied.

Step Five:

This step will help you clean your hard drive. Because each computer is different, the steps may vary for you. Typically disk cleanup is the term you're looking for and can be found under accessories or system tools.

Cell Phone

If you have a smartphone, you know how annoying it is to receive a no more storage alert. The alert always seems to appear when you're trying to take an important picture. The alert makes you miss the shot or requires you to delete valuable items in a hurry. With the steps below, you can avoid this problem and keep your phone running as fast as possible!

Step One:

The first step is to delete apps you don't regularly use. This can usually be done by pressing your finger on the icon for a few seconds. A small x should appear in the corner of the app to help you delete it. Deleting unused apps will not only free up storage space, but will save you time looking for the apps you actually use.

Step Two:

The next step is to delete apps that aren't adding any value to your life. Facebook, Instagram, and Snapchat can be great, but if they aren't uplifting you or helping you in any way, it's time to delete them. This step is about decluttering and clearing your mindset, so keep that in mind when sifting through apps.

Step Three:

Go through all of your downloaded music and movies. If you have made purchases, you can always redownload them so no need to worry. Music and movies take up a lot of storage space on your phone and can actually slow the device down drastically.

Step Four:

Delete photos that aren't serving a purpose. Many photos are great to keep and look at during free time or during a tough day. However, most of us are carrying around photos that were taken accidently, multiple shots of the same photo, or photos that are already being stored elsewhere. Old photos should be moved to a cloud service or hard drive to make room for new photos.

Step Five:

This step will help you get rid of annoying notifications that interrupt your day. Sure, it's great to get alerts from your favorite sport's apps, messages, or Facebook, but many apps send you useless notifications to simply let you know they're there. In the settings of your device, locate notifications and turn off the notifications from apps that aren't giving useful information.

<u>Step Six:</u>

If you find yourself getting distracted easily by your phone, monitor how much you use your phone. This step has more to do with organizing and decluttering your brain. Believe it or not, your phone can overwhelm you and cause headaches. If this scenario sounds like it's relevant to you, monitor your phone use for a more enjoyable day or evening.

Top 10 Declutter and Organization Apps

The apps listed below will help you manage everyday tasks and keep your life more organized. According to O, The Oprah Magazine (2019), these are the top 10 apps of 2019 that will make your life easier. Take a look and see if any are right for you!

1. ***Wunderlist***

This app specializes in to-do lists. If you have multiple lists, this app is the one for you! It's easy to use, and its great design will help you accomplish all of your tasks. You can set reminders, make notes, and record voice memos. This app is perfect for personal use and for work-related business.

2. ***Calendly***

This app specializes in helping you manage your time and serves as a productivity coach. This app will help you organize your calendar and ensure you're never double booked.

3. ***CamCard***

This app will help you keep track of contracts for personal use and business. In addition, the scanning feature of this app will help you organize business cards and transfer the information into an electronic address book.

4. ***Time Timer***

This app gives a useful graphic to show you how much time is passing, and how much time is left within the hour. If this motivates you to get your work done, then give this app a try!

5. ***LastPass***

This app will help you manage the passwords for all your accounts. Both work and personal passwords can be safely stored in this app. The time consuming "forgot my password" steps can be a thing of the past.

6. *Evernote*

This app will help you organize your thoughts and notes. You can manage to-do lists, business cards, receipts, documents, and notes using this app.

7. *Jour*

This app specializes in decreasing distractions and will help you focus on getting more work done efficiently. This app is great for your mental health and will help you channel any negative thoughts out so you can focus on other projects. A daily planner is given to help you prioritize your emotions and wellbeing.

8. *Todoist*

This app is another to-do list organizer that allows you to set alarms, task due dates, and manage projects. This is a great way to keep everything in one place.

9. *ActiveInbox*

This app will help you prioritize your emails. The app integrates into your mailbox and takes any emails that require action, and turns them into easy to follow tasks. This will help you see your to-do list without having to open and sort through each email.

10. Postmates

This app will help busy individuals who don't have time for meal planning. The app helps you plan out meals and will help you find delivery spots when you don't have the time to make your own food.

Conclusion

For many, cleaning and organizing a home can be an incredibly hard task. With busy lives and long workdays, don't look forward to coming home and cleaning their house. When a home is neglected, over time the home can become filled with clutter that causes stress and crowded storage spaces. Finding items takes longer and is stressful due to the overflow of items.

Although homes need to be maintained and well kept, with the help of this guide, home cleaning and decluttering no longer needs to be a dreaded thought. When a home is clean and organized, proper rest and relaxation takes place. Having a beautiful space will help you unwind after a long week at work and time can be spent enjoying other activities like hanging out with loved ones.

Having a clean home might require you to start with a deep clean. Fortunately, this guide has different, customizable lists that will help you clean areas of your home as efficiently as possible. The guide goes through each room and gives specific instructions on the different items and furniture that need to be cleaned. These tips will stay with you long after reading this guide and after some practice, you will be able to confidently clean your home without any help. At the end of each section, a checklist was given to guide you through different activities and the order they should be performed.

After you have successfully cleaned your home, decluttering and organization can take place. Having a good system will save you time looking for items and will help keep your space clean. This guide has tips for each room and suggestions on how to make the most of your space. If you live in a small apartment or home, these tips will come in handy as some teach you how to create more space. Many items can be stored in a helpful way, but also add a nice design element to the room. This guide will help you decide what to keep and what to get rid of. Each section will help make your space spectacular by cleaning, decluttering, and organizing your belongings.

To help you through the cleaning and decluttering process, other helpful lists have been given to you in this guide. Everyone has a different way of cleaning and these lists will help you to fit cleaning and organization tasks into your schedule. Whether you prefer cleaning on a weekly or monthly basis, there are helpful lists for both. In addition, a yearly list has been given to you to help you deep clean different areas of the home throughout the year. This will prevent you from having to do one large deep clean if that's not preferred or possible.

In addition to cleaning and decluttering lists, information about different cleaners has been provided as well. Natural cleaners have become popular over the last decade and for good reason. Scientists have linked the chemicals found in many cleaners to various health problems. By using toxic cleaners, not only are you unknowingly harming your health but also the health of your children and family. Toxic cleaners also have the ability to harm the environment and research has shown its negative impacts. Toxic cleaners should be avoided and this guide will provide wonderful alternatives that are safe for you and the whole family. Not only are these cleaners affordable, but you likely already have the ingredients needed right in your home.

By following the suggestions in this guide, you can look forward to a clean and decluttered environment. After reading this guide, you'll be well prepared and know how to maintain the hard work you put into your home. With this information and helpful tips, you'll no longer dread cleaning your home and will be able to develop quick routines. Your home will stay clean and organized, and you'll have more time to do what you love, with the people you love!

If this book was helpful to you and you enjoyed the style, take 5 minutes of your time to let me know what you think with a short review on Amazon. Good luck on your journey to a more spacious and joyful home.

Printed in Great Britain
by Amazon